The Black Book of Capitalism: Global Manipulation and Human Exploitation

Carmellini Duarte

CHAPTER 1: THE ROOTS OF CAPITALISM – FROM BARTER TO THE FIRST COINS

Before the advent of capitalism, human societies operated under vastly different economic systems. Barter, or the direct exchange of goods and services, was one of the earliest forms of trade. Over time, the growing complexity of transactions and the need for a more efficient medium of exchange led to the invention of the first coins, planting the seeds for the conception of capitalism that would shape the modern world.

The Barter System: The Beginnings of Economic Exchange

In primitive societies, barter was the primary form of trade. People directly exchanged goods or services based on their needs. For example, one might trade food for tools or clothing. Although simple, barter presented clear limitations:

- **Coincidence of wants:** For an exchange to occur, both parties had to want exactly what the other offered.
- **Difficulty in measuring value:** There was no standard to determine if a sack of grain was worth more or less than an axe, for example.

These challenges drove the search for a more practical system, ultimately leading to the creation of a universal medium of exchange: the first coins.

The Emergence of Coins and the Evolution of Trade

The earliest coins appeared around 3,000 BCE in Mesopotamia, where precious metals like gold and silver began to be used as standards of exchange. These metals were valuable, durable, and portable, making them ideal replacements for the barter system.

Later, in the 7th century BCE, the Kingdom of Lydia (modern-day Turkey) introduced the first minted coins, made of a gold and silver alloy called electrum. These coins had value guaranteed by the state authority and quickly spread across Europe and Asia, revolutionizing economic exchange.

The introduction of coins enabled the creation of broader and more complex markets where the value of goods was measured in money. This development was instrumental in the rise of city-states and the first trade-based economies.

From the Middle Ages to Capitalism: The Role of Corporations and Banks

During the Middle Ages, feudalism was the dominant system in Europe. The economy was land-based, and production primarily served local consumption. Most people lived as serfs or peasants, working lands owned by the nobility.

However, between the 11th and 15th centuries, significant changes began to transform this model:

1. **Growth of cities:** Urban revival brought local markets, fairs, and international trade routes, encouraging the circulation of money.

2. **The rise of commercial corporations:** Organizations like the Hanseatic League in Europe began dominating maritime trade, setting standards for contracts, pricing, and the transport of goods.

3. **The emergence of banks:** Banking institutions, such as those of the Medici family in Italy, revolutionized the concept of credit, enabling large-scale loans and investments.

These changes laid the foundation for capitalism, introducing concepts such as profit, wealth accumulation, and reinvestment in commerce.

The Father of Capitalism: Adam Smith and the Conception of the System

Although capitalism has deep historical roots, its theoretical framework only emerged in the 18th century with Scottish philosopher Adam Smith. In his book *The Wealth of Nations*

(1776), Smith outlined the fundamental principles that would define the capitalist system:

- **The invisible hand of the market:** Smith believed that individual pursuit of profit would benefit society as a whole, naturally and efficiently guiding markets.
- **Division of labor:** He emphasized how specialization increased productivity, making work more efficient.
- **Free trade and competition:** Smith advocated for markets operating without government interference, allowing competition to regulate prices and product quality.

While Adam Smith is often called the "father of capitalism," his ideas reflected practices already developing. He codified these observations, shaping the intellectual foundation of a system that would dominate the world in the centuries to come.

The Initial Conception of Capitalism

At its core, capitalism emerged as an economic system built on three fundamental pillars:

1. **Private property:** The idea that individuals can own assets and means of production.
2. **Capital accumulation:** Wealth generated should be reinvested to create even more wealth.
3. **Profit as motivation:** Economic transactions were driven by the pursuit of profit, making financial gain the primary objective.

These concepts marked a radical departure from barter and feudalism, signaling the beginning of a new economic era.

Conclusion: The Embryo of a Global System

Capitalism began to take shape long before it was formally named. It arose from humanity's need to overcome the limitations of barter and the relentless pursuit of efficiency and wealth. The introduction of early currency, the growth of cities, and the development of banks and commercial corporations paved the way for a system that would come to dominate the world.

In the next chapter, we will delve into how mercantilism—the first practical stage of capitalism—consolidated these principles, expanding trade and shaping global economies.

CHAPTER 2: THE BIRTH OF CAPITALISM IN MERCANTILISM

Capitalism, as the dominant economic system, did not emerge overnight. It evolved gradually over centuries, originating from economic practices that began consolidating in medieval Europe and reached their peak during the period known as mercantilism. This chapter explores the roots of this system, uncovering how the accumulation of wealth and the control of global markets laid the foundation for modern capitalism.

The Rise of Mercantilism

Between the 15th and 18th centuries, mercantilism became the predominant economic model in Europe. It was characterized by the belief that a nation's wealth depended on the accumulation of precious metals, such as gold and silver, and the relentless pursuit of a favorable trade balance—exporting more than importing.

Governments of the time viewed trade as a zero-sum game: for one country to gain, another had to lose. This mentality led to the centralization of economic power within the state, which began to intervene directly in trade by supporting monopolies and colonial endeavors to secure competitive advantages.

The Role of the Age of Exploration

Mercantilism thrived due to the Age of Exploration. Driven by advances in navigation, such as the compass and caravels, powers like Portugal, Spain, England, France, and the Netherlands embarked on maritime expeditions in search of new trade routes, spices, gold, and territories.

1. **The Plundering of Colonies**

   Mercantilism depended heavily on the exploitation of colonies. The Americas, Africa, and Asia became inexhaustible sources of wealth for European nations.

Minerals, timber, spices, sugar, and other resources were extracted on a massive scale and sent to the metropoles.

This exploitation extended beyond natural resources: millions of people were enslaved and transported to serve mercantilist interests. The violence and genocide inflicted on the colonies remain indelible marks on the early stages of capitalism.

2. **Commercial Monopolies**

   Companies like the Dutch and British East India Companies became symbols of mercantilist power. These corporations, often supported by military force, monopolized trade routes and exploited colonies. Their relentless pursuit of profit solidified the notion that capital should be used to generate more capital—a central tenet of capitalism.

The State as the Engine of the Economy

Under mercantilism, the state played a crucial role in the economy, a stark contrast to the liberal ideals of late-stage capitalism. Governments not only regulated markets but also directly invested in colonial expansion and the strengthening of local industries.

European kings and nobles financed maritime expeditions and provided incentives to merchants and manufacturers. Protectionist policies, with high tariffs on imports, aimed to bolster domestic production and keep wealth within the nation.

The Economic and Social Legacy of Mercantilism

Although mercantilism was gradually replaced by economic liberalism, its influence on the birth of capitalism is undeniable. It established fundamental pillars such as:

- **Capital accumulation**: Wealth generated through colonial plunder and monopolized trade created the first major private and national fortunes.
- **Global connections**: Mercantilism consolidated the earliest global economic networks, linking markets

across continents.

- **Systematic exploitation**: The use of enslaved labor, resource extraction, and destruction of local cultures shaped a pattern of predatory practices that persist in modern capitalism.

Conclusion: The First Step of a Global System

Mercantilism was not merely an early phase of capitalism but a laboratory where the foundations of the system were tested. The insatiable desire to accumulate wealth, combined with the exploitation of lands and people, paved the way for the capitalist model we know today.

In the next chapter, we will explore how the Industrial Revolution marked the next step in this transformation, introducing an even greater scale of exploitation and wealth accumulation.

CHAPTER 3: THE IMPACT OF THE INDUSTRIAL REVOLUTION

The Industrial Revolution marked one of the most transformative moments in human history. Beginning in the late 18th century, primarily in England, it not only profoundly altered the global economy but also triggered social, political, and environmental changes that shaped the modern world. This chapter examines the impact of this phenomenon, revealing how it accelerated the foundations of capitalism and entrenched economic inequality.

The Machine Revolution: A New Model of Production

The defining feature of the Industrial Revolution was the replacement of manual labor with machines. Innovations such as the steam engine, mechanical loom, and internal combustion engine revolutionized industries like textiles, metallurgy, and transportation.

Before the Revolution, production was artisanal and decentralized, limited to local needs. With mechanization, several changes emerged:

1. **Mass production**: Goods began to be manufactured in large quantities, reducing costs and increasing supply.
2. **The rise of factories**: Industries centralized production, drawing workers into urban centers and transforming the rural economy.

This new organization of labor became one of the pillars of capitalism, enabling wealth accumulation on an unprecedented scale.

Social Transformations: The Rise of the Proletariat

The Industrial Revolution also drastically reshaped social structures. Millions of people left the countryside to work in cities, forming the working class. However, this transition brought numerous challenges:

- **Inhumane working conditions**: Workers endured up to 16-hour shifts in unsafe factories, with no labor rights.
- **Child labor**: Children were frequently exploited, earning meager wages for grueling hours.
- **Social inequality**: While the industrial bourgeoisie amassed fortunes, the working class lived in dire poverty, crammed into overcrowded, unsanitary urban neighborhoods.

Uncontrolled urbanization led to rising crime rates, poverty, and infant mortality, exposing the human cost of rapid industrialization.

Economic Impacts: Expansion and Exploitation

The Industrial Revolution solidified capitalism as the dominant economic system. Businesses sought to maximize profits, leading to:

1. **Imperialist expansion**: Industrialized nations like England and France colonized vast regions of Asia, Africa, and the Americas in search of raw materials and consumer markets.
2. **Natural resource exploitation**: Intensive mining and deforestation became common practices, causing environmental degradation.
3. **Creation of monopolies**: Giant corporations began to dominate entire economic sectors, stifling competition.

This model generated unprecedented wealth for a few, while the majority of the population remained marginalized.

Environmental Impacts: The Price of Progress

The Industrial Revolution also marked the beginning of the modern environmental crisis. The intensive use of coal and other fossil fuels:

- Drastically increased emissions of pollutants, contributing to climate change.
- Contaminated rivers and soils, affecting entire ecosystems.
- Created highly polluted cities, such as London, where factory smoke caused widespread respiratory problems.

These issues, though largely ignored at the time, are direct consequences of the capitalist pursuit of efficiency and profit.

The Industrial Revolution and Growing Inequality

While it boosted the global economy, the Industrial Revolution deepened economic inequality. Industrialized nations grew wealthier at the expense of exploited colonies and workers, creating a divide between the Global North and South that persists to this day.

At the same time, within industrialized societies, the gap between rich and poor widened, with factory owners amassing fortunes while workers barely survived.

Conclusion: The Revolution That Changed Everything

The Industrial Revolution was a watershed moment in human history, marking the advent of industrialized capitalism that shaped the 19th century and beyond. However, its impacts — from labor and resource exploitation to environmental degradation — reveal the darker side of this "progress."

CHAPTER 4: HOW CAPITALISM BECAME DOMINANT WORLDWIDE

Capitalism did not emerge as the global economic system we know today. It was shaped and driven by centuries of economic, political, and social transformations that culminated in its worldwide dominance. This chapter explores the events and factors that solidified capitalism as the driving force of the global economy, from the era of mercantilist empires to the present day.

From Mercantilism to Modern Capitalism

Mercantilism, the predominant economic system between the 16th and 18th centuries, was a direct precursor to capitalism. Supported by the state, European nations sought to accumulate wealth through international trade, establishing colonies and monopolizing resources.

Key elements connecting mercantilism to capitalism include:

- **Capital accumulation:** Colonies were exploited to generate wealth that fueled the growth of European economies.

- **Emergence of large trading corporations:** Companies such as the East India Company established commercial practices that became central to capitalism.

- **Expansion of global markets:** The creation of intercontinental trade routes paved the way for economic globalization.

These foundations were deepened by the Industrial Revolution, which accelerated mass production and urbanization, cementing capitalism as the dominant system.

The Rise of Economic Liberalism

In the 18th century, Enlightenment ideals fostered economic liberalism, a philosophy that challenged state control over the economy by advocating for free markets and competition. Adam Smith, with his seminal work *The Wealth of Nations* (1776), played a pivotal role in providing the theoretical framework for capitalism:

- **Free market:** The idea that the economy thrives when individuals pursue their self-interest.
- **Limited government intervention:** Smith argued that governments should restrict their role in the economy, allowing the market to regulate itself.

These principles became the foundation of modern capitalism, particularly with the rise of Western economies in the 19th century.

Imperialism and the Globalization of Capitalism

During the 19th and 20th centuries, imperialism became a primary driver of capitalist expansion. Industrialized nations sought territories in Asia, Africa, and Latin America, using these regions as sources of cheap raw materials and markets for their manufactured goods.

The impact of imperialism on the globalization of capitalism includes:

1. **Destruction of local economies:** Many traditional economies were replaced by the production of goods for the global market, such as cotton, rubber, and coffee.

2. **Exploitation of labor and resources:** Colonizers relied on cheap and often forced labor, perpetuating economic inequalities.

3. **Forced integration into the capitalist system:** Even after the end of formal colonialism, many nations remained dependent on Western economies, now under the model of neocolonialism.

The Role of the United States and Contemporary Capitalism

In the 20th century, the United States emerged as the leading global capitalist power, especially after World War II. Its influence was solidified through:

- **The Marshall Plan:** The reconstruction of war-torn Europe was financed by the U.S., ensuring the adoption of capitalist economic models in the beneficiary countries.
- **The Cold War:** The ideological battle between capitalism and communism promoted capitalism as synonymous with freedom and prosperity.
- **International institutions:** Organizations such as the International Monetary Fund (IMF) and the World Bank were established to expand capitalism globally, often imposing neoliberal reforms on developing countries.

Neoliberalism: The Global Consolidation of Capitalism

In the 1980s, neoliberalism solidified capitalism's dominance. Championed by figures like Margaret Thatcher in the United Kingdom and Ronald Reagan in the U.S., neoliberalism advocated:

1. **Privatizations:** Public enterprises were sold to the private sector, reducing the state's role in the economy.
2. **Deregulation:** Laws protecting workers and the environment were relaxed to encourage business growth.
3. **Economic globalization:** International trade and capital flows were facilitated, further integrating world economies.

These policies deepened economic inequality and the exploitation of peripheral countries while cementing capitalism as the dominant economic system.

Capitalism in the Digital Era

In the 21st century, capitalism adapted to the digital age, driven by technological innovation and globalization:

- **Tech giants:** Companies like Amazon, Apple, and Google became symbols of modern capitalism, amassing unprecedented wealth.
- **The attention economy:** Platforms like social media transformed human attention into a valuable product, exploiting personal data to maximize profits.
- **Rising inequality:** Despite technological advancements, wealth concentration in the hands of a few has intensified.

Conclusion: The System That Conquered the World

Capitalism became dominant over the centuries through its ability to adapt and expand, leveraging innovations, conflicts, and social changes. From the first coins to tech giants, the system has shaped the modern world, driving remarkable advancements while perpetuating inequality and exploitation.

CHAPTER 5: THE MAIN PROBLEMS AND DAMAGES OF CAPITALISM UNTIL THE INDUSTRIAL REVOLUTION

Since its origins, capitalism has left a trail of profound transformations in society but also brought with it a series of problems that devastated humanity. This chapter analyzes the key negative impacts of the capitalist system up until the 19th century, highlighting how its relentless pursuit of profit led to exploitation, violence, inequality, and social degradation.

1. EXPLOITATION OF LABOR AND INHUMANE CONDITIONS

From the beginning, capitalism relied on the extreme exploitation of labor. During mercantilism and later with the Industrial Revolution, workers were subjected to cruel conditions:

- **Exhausting work shifts:** Workers often spent up to 16 hours a day in unhealthy factories.
- **Child labor:** Children, sometimes as young as 5 years old, were exploited in mines and factories.
- **Lack of rights:** There were no regulations to ensure safety, fair wages, or protection against abuse.

These conditions resulted in high rates of accidents, diseases, and deaths, leaving entire communities in misery.

2. SLAVERY AND HUMAN TRAFFICKING

Mercantile capitalism heavily relied on slavery to accumulate wealth. Millions of Africans were kidnapped, sold, and transported in inhumane conditions to work in colonies around the world.

Key Consequences:

- **Dehumanization:** Enslaved individuals were treated as commodities, evaluated by physical strength and work capacity.
- **Cultural genocide:** Entire peoples had their traditions and identities erased.
- **Profit from suffering:** European banks, insurers, and merchants enriched themselves at the cost of slavery.

Headlines and Relevant Historical Facts:

- *"The Slave Ship 'Zong' Throws 132 Enslaved People Overboard to Profit from Insurance"* (1781).
- *"Thousands Die in Caribbean Sugar Plantations."*

3. WARS AND CONFLICTS FOR WEALTH ACCUMULATION

Capitalism has been at the root of various wars and conflicts, driven by competition between European powers for resources and markets.

- **Colonial wars:** Nations like England, France, Spain, and Portugal waged violent battles to dominate territories in Africa, Asia, and the Americas.
- **Indigenous genocides:** Native peoples were exterminated to make way for the exploitation of land and resources.

Headlines or Significant Events:

- *"The Spanish Massacred the Aztec and Inca Peoples for Gold and Silver."*
- *"The Dutch and the English Fight for Monopoly in the East Indies."*

These wars generated enormous profits for European bourgeoisie while millions were killed or displaced from their lands.

4. EARLY ENVIRONMENTAL DEGRADATION

Capitalist exploitation of natural resources began long before the Industrial Revolution but was exacerbated by it.

- **Deforestation:** Entire forests were destroyed for agriculture and timber exploitation.
- **Pollution:** With the Industrial Revolution, rivers and the air began to be contaminated by factories.
- **Soil exhaustion:** Intensive agricultural practices destroyed fertile land.

Headlines or Relevant Episodes:

- *"Manchester Factories Cover the City in Black Soot" (19th century).*
- *"Inland English Rivers Turned into Sewers by Industries."*

5. GROWING ECONOMIC INEQUALITY

Capitalism created an economic elite that controlled most of the wealth, while the majority of the population lived in poverty.

- **Capital accumulation:** The rich became richer, while workers barely survived.
- **Poor urbanization:** Cities grew without planning, with millions living in slums and overcrowded tenements.

Headlines or Examples:

- *"Families Live on Less than a Weekly Salary While Employers Build Mansions" (London, 1850).*
- *"The Weavers' Revolt: Workers Destroy Machines in Protest Against Low Wages" (England, early 19th century).*

6. REVOLTS AND STRUGGLES AGAINST THE SYSTEM

From the beginning, there was resistance to capitalism. Workers, enslaved people, and indigenous communities fought against exploitation:

- **Slave revolts:** Such as Spartacus' Revolt in ancient Rome and Toussaint Louverture's revolt in Haiti, which led to the country's independence.

- **Labor movements:** In the 19th century, unions began to organize, demanding better working conditions and fair wages.

These struggles exposed the brutality of capitalism but were also harshly suppressed, with leaders executed and protests violently quelled.

CONCLUSION: THE TRAIL OF DEVASTATION

By the time of the Industrial Revolution, capitalism left a legacy marked by exploitation, violence, and inequality. Although it propelled trade and innovation, the human and environmental costs were immense. Millions suffered and died in the pursuit of wealth accumulation, while the system solidified itself as the dominant force in the world.

CHAPTER 6: WARS FOR PROFIT

Since its emergence, capitalism has shown an unsettling characteristic: the ability to transform war into a tool for economic expansion. Conflicts that could have religious, political, or territorial causes came to be shaped by economic interests, while millions of lives were sacrificed to fuel the engine of wealth accumulation. This chapter analyzes how capitalism used armed conflict to solidify itself, bringing destruction and inequality under the pretense of progress.

1. THE COLONIAL SYSTEM AND WARS FOR WEALTH

The European powers of the mercantile period engaged in violent disputes to control territories rich in natural resources. These wars marked the beginning of an era where profit took precedence over human dignity.

- **Extermination of Indigenous Peoples:** In the Americas, Africa, Asia, and Oceania, entire communities were decimated to allow colonizers to exploit gold, silver, spices, and other valuable resources.

- **The Race for Precious Metals:** Expeditions such as those led by Hernán Cortés and Francisco Pizarro destroyed entire civilizations— the Aztecs, Mayans, and Incas—to fill the coffers of European crowns.

Notable Example:

- The Spanish conquest of the Americas generated a massive flow of silver to Europe but at the cost of genocides, slavery, and cultural destruction.

2. THE SLAVE TRADE AND WARS IN AFRICA

Slavery, a central element of the emerging capitalist system, fueled wars within the African continent. European merchants encouraged local tribes to capture rivals to sell them as enslaved people.

- **Commercially Driven Conflicts:** Weapons and financial incentives were offered to tribal leaders to encourage wars that increased the number of captives available for the transatlantic trade.

- **Profit Over Humanity:** Each enslaved person represented a lucrative investment for European merchants, banks, and insurance companies.

Historical Event:

- The massacre on the slave ship *Zong* in 1781 exemplifies the system's cruelty: 132 enslaved Africans were thrown overboard so the crew could claim insurance for "losses."

3. TRADE DISPUTES AND THE RISE OF IMPERIALISM

As capitalism evolved, controlling markets and trade routes became a strategic goal for European nations, leading to wars that, while disguised as political disputes, were essentially driven by economic motives.

- **Anglo-Dutch Wars (17th and 18th centuries):** Conflicts between England and the Netherlands over maritime trade dominance and colonies.

- **Napoleonic Wars (1803–1815):** Beyond their ideological aspects, these conflicts sought to consolidate France's economic power while creating opportunities for arms trade and loans among allies and adversaries.

4. THE ROLE OF CORPORATIONS AND BANKS

From the outset, companies and financial institutions were central players in armed conflicts, often acting as initiators or financiers of wars.

- **East India Companies:** The English and Dutch East India Companies maintained private armies, waging wars to monopolize trade in spices, tea, and other products.
- **The Role of Banks:** European banks, such as those in Amsterdam and London, financed expeditions and conflicts, profiting through interest and speculation.

Historical Example:

- The Royal African Company was established to exploit the slave trade, profiting from war and the capture of people in Africa.

5. THE HUMAN AND ENVIRONMENTAL COST

Wars waged in the pursuit of profit were not limited to the loss of human lives; they also left a legacy of environmental destruction and structural inequality.

- **Destruction of Communities and Cultures:** Indigenous and African peoples were exterminated or subjugated, losing land, identity, and basic rights.
- **Environmental Exploitation:** Forests, soil, and ecosystems were devastated to extract resources such as gold, silver, spices, and timber.
- **Creation of Persistent Inequalities:** Colonial powers accumulated wealth while leaving their colonies in poverty and underdevelopment—an inheritance that persists today.

Alarming Data:

- It is estimated that between the 16th and 19th centuries, over 12 million Africans were captured and enslaved, with millions dying during the Atlantic crossing or in American plantations.

6. WAR AS AN ECONOMIC MODEL

Even after the 19th century, wars continued to be used as an economic tool by capitalism. Although this chapter focuses on events before the Industrial Revolution, the "war-for-profit" logic remains relevant today.

Modern Example:

- The dispute over oil and other natural resources in the Middle East highlights how capitalism still uses armed conflict to maintain global dominance.

CONCLUSION

Wars waged in the name of profit represent one of the darkest legacies of capitalism. The relentless pursuit of wealth transformed armed conflicts into a profitable business, where human lives and ecosystems were treated as mere commodities. These practices laid the foundations for inequalities and crises that continue to haunt the world today.

CHAPTER 7: THE OPIUM WAR AND THE EXPLOITATION OF CHINA

In the 19th century, China, with its rich culture, self-sufficient economy, and vast resources, became the target of one of history's most cruel and destructive capitalist exploitation campaigns: the Opium Wars. Orchestrated primarily by the British Empire, these wars reveal how capitalism employed inhuman strategies to dominate markets and subjugate peoples, transforming trade into a tool of social and cultural destruction.

1. The Context: China Before Opium

For centuries, China was one of the world's largest economic powers, exporting silk, porcelain, and tea in exchange for silver. However, this balance disturbed Western powers, particularly Britain, which faced a trade deficit due to high demand for Chinese goods and low acceptance of British products in the Chinese market.

- **The Tea Monopoly**: China completely controlled the tea trade, a product of immense importance to the British.
- **Resistance to Western Capitalism**: The Qing dynasty restricted trade with foreigners, maintaining a closed and sovereign economy.

2. The Introduction of Opium

To reverse the trade imbalance, the British East India Company began trafficking opium from India to China. Despite being illegal in China, opium became a tool to weaken Chinese society and open the market to Western exploitation.

- **The Effects of Addiction**: Millions of Chinese people were devastated by opium consumption, resulting in an unprecedented social crisis. Families were destroyed, workers abandoned their jobs, and entire communities succumbed to addiction.

- **Profit Over Morality**: For the British, opium trafficking was highly profitable, fueling both trade and colonial expansion.

3. The First Opium War (1839–1842)

In 1839, the Chinese government, led by Commissioner Lin Zexu, launched a campaign against the opium trade by confiscating and destroying large shipments of the drug. This measure challenged British economic interests and sparked the First Opium War.

- **British Military Superiority**: Equipped with advanced naval technology and modern weapons, the British forces easily defeated the Chinese troops, imposing a humiliating agreement.
- **The Treaty of Nanjing (1842)**: China was forced to cede Hong Kong to the British, open five ports to foreign trade, and pay massive indemnities.

4. The Second Opium War (1856–1860)

The humiliation of the First War did not fully satisfy Western interests. In 1856, a new dispute known as the Second Opium War erupted, led by Britain and France, with support from other Western nations.

- **Imperialist Demands**: Western powers demanded greater access to trade, legalization of opium, and freedom for Christian missionaries.
- **The Plundering of the Summer Palace**: In 1860, Anglo-French forces looted and burned the magnificent Summer Palace in Beijing, a symbol of Chinese culture and sovereignty.

5. The Consequences of Exploitation

The Opium Wars left deep scars in China, transforming it into a semi-subjugated nation exploited by foreign powers.

- **Economic Destruction**: Forced trade and financial indemnities significantly weakened the Chinese economy.
- **Social Decline**: Millions of people became addicted to opium, exacerbating poverty and instability.
- **The Era of Unequal Treaties**: Under military and economic

pressure, China was forced to sign a series of treaties that exclusively favored Western interests, including the opening of additional ports and the ceding of more territories.

6. Capitalism's Role in China's Devastation

The Opium Wars illustrate how capitalism, in its pursuit of profit at any cost, can destroy entire nations. The opium trade was driven not only by imperial greed but also by the capitalist logic of continuous expansion and profit maximization.

- **Human Impact Ignored**: Capitalist exploitation treated the Chinese population as disposable tools in a profit-driven scheme.
- **The Logic of Economic Domination**: For British capitalism, dominating the Chinese market was crucial to strengthening global hegemony.

7. Lessons and Legacy

The Opium Wars not only mark a dark chapter in Chinese history but also offer crucial lessons about the consequences of unregulated capitalism.

- **Global Inequality**: The exploitation of China highlighted how Western capitalism depended on subjugating other nations.
- **Cultural Resistance**: Despite the destruction, China preserved parts of its cultural identity, which would later inspire movements of renewal and revolution.
- **A Historical Warning**: The devastation caused by the Opium Wars serves as a reminder of the atrocities that can occur when profit is placed above humanity.

CONCLUSION

The Opium Wars demonstrate how capitalism aligns with imperialism to exploit nations and peoples for the benefit of the few. The suffering China endured during this period was not an accident but a direct consequence of a system that prioritizes wealth over human lives. In the next chapter, we will explore another episode of exploitation and expansion: the impact of the Industrial Revolution on the capitalist world.

CHAPTER 8: COLONIAL WARS AND THE PLUNDERING OF NATURAL RESOURCES

Throughout the centuries, colonialism and capitalism intertwined in a devastating way. In their relentless pursuit of profit and control, imperial powers did not hesitate to wage wars and exploit entire populations to obtain valuable natural resources. These conflicts, marked by brutality and cultural and environmental destruction, shaped world history and paved the way for global capitalist dominance.

1. COLONIALISM AND ITS CAPITALIST FOUNDATIONS

Since the beginning of the Age of Exploration, European powers sought to expand their territories to control lands rich in resources such as gold, silver, spices, timber, and, later, oil and industrial minerals.

- **The Profit Logic**: Colonies were seen as sources of cheap raw materials and captive markets for manufactured goods, forming a highly profitable economic cycle for the metropolises.

- **Structural Inequality**: The colonial system depended on the intensive exploitation of local labor and the expropriation of indigenous lands.

2. COLONIAL WARS: THE VIOLENCE OF EXPANSION

The Conquest of the Americas (15th-17th centuries)

The arrival of Europeans in the Americas resulted in genocide, enslavement, and the displacement of indigenous populations. The goal was clear: extract natural resources, such as gold and silver, at any cost.

- **The Exploitation of Potosí**: The silver mine at Potosí, in present-day Bolivia, became a symbol of capitalist greed. Millions of indigenous and enslaved African people died in brutal conditions to enrich Europe.
- **The Plundering of the Aztecs and Incas**: Entire civilizations were destroyed, and their riches were sent to European coffers.

The Colonization of Africa (19th-20th centuries)

Known as the "Scramble for Africa," the division of the continent among European powers led to wars, massacres, and the plundering of natural resources such as diamonds, gold, and rubber.

- **The Congo Free State**: Under the personal reign of King Leopold II of Belgium, millions of Congolese people died in forced labor for rubber and ivory extraction.
- **Economic Apartheid**: The exploitation of South African gold and diamond mines financed European wealth while keeping Africans in poverty and under oppressive regimes.

Middle Eastern Wars and Oil (20th-21st centuries)

With the discovery of oil, the Middle East became a battlefield for capitalist powers seeking control over this strategic wealth.

- **Artificial Conflicts**: The manipulation of borders and alliances fueled civil wars and instability, benefiting Western corporations.
- **The Gulf War (1990-1991)**: A prime example of how capitalism prioritized control over natural resources under the pretext of defending freedom and democracy.

3. ENVIRONMENTAL AND LOCAL POPULATION IMPACT

Environmental Devastation

The unrestrained extraction of natural resources devastated ecosystems worldwide.

- **Amazon Deforestation**: During colonization, vast areas were destroyed to create monocultures such as sugarcane.

- **Predatory Mining**: River and land contamination was common in mineral-rich regions, like Africa and Latin America.

Destruction of Cultures and Ways of Life

Indigenous and local populations were systematically removed or exterminated to make way for capitalist exploitation.

- **Ethnocide**: Traditions and languages disappeared under the imposition of foreign cultures.

- **Enslavement and Servitude**: Millions of people were forced to work in inhumane conditions, laying the foundations for colonial fortunes.

4. GLOBAL CONSEQUENCES

Colonial wars and the plundering of natural resources created profound and lasting inequalities:

- **Endemic Poverty**: Many post-colonial countries remain economically dependent on raw material exports, suffering from unfair global market prices.

- **Ongoing Conflicts**: The artificial borders drawn by colonial powers generated ethnic and territorial disputes that persist to this day.

- **Economic Domination**: Multinational corporations inherited control over natural resources, perpetuating the legacy of colonial exploitation.

5. THE ROLE OF CAPITALISM IN COLONIALISM

Colonialism was not only a political or military phenomenon but also an economic strategy grounded in the capitalist principles of accumulation and expansion.

- **Exploitation as an Economic Engine**: Without the plundering of natural resources, Western capitalism would not have achieved global dominance.
- **The Human Cost**: While the elites enriched themselves, billions of people faced poverty, oppression, and death.

6. REFLECTIONS AND LEGACIES

Colonialism and the wars associated with it left indelible marks on human history.

- **A Historical Debt**: Nations that enriched themselves through colonial exploitation have yet to fully address the damages caused.

- **Perpetuation of Exploitation**: Even after independence, many countries remain trapped in neocolonial economic structures dominated by global capitalist interests.

CONCLUSION

Colonial wars and the plundering of natural resources exemplify the brutal face of capitalism: the ruthless exploitation of lands and peoples to enrich a minority. In the next chapter, we will examine how the Industrial Revolution intensified this logic, consolidating capitalism as the dominant system and expanding its devastating impacts even further.

CHAPTER 9: THE PROFIT OF COLONIAL POWERS FROM THE SUFFERING AND EXPLOITATION OF COLONIES

Colonialism was not just about territorial dominance; it was an economic system based on the suffering of millions of people and the destruction of cultures and ecosystems. Among the colonizing nations, Portugal and Spain stood out, particularly in their exploitation of Brazil. While these empires enriched themselves through the plundering of natural resources and the exploitation of enslaved labor, the legacies of their actions still resonate today, with a lingering relationship of disdain and indifference toward the countries they once dominated.

1. BRAZIL AS A SOURCE OF WEALTH FOR PORTUGAL AND SPAIN

When Portugal and Spain established dominance over the Americas, Brazil became one of the most valuable colonies of the Portuguese Empire. Over the centuries, Brazil was exploited to enrich Portugal and, to a lesser extent, Spain, which, through the Treaty of Tordesillas (1494), also benefited from a portion of South America's riches.

Portugal, Gold, and Sugar: The Wealth that Sustained the Empire

- **Sugar:** The sugar cycle was the first major economic driver of colonial Brazil. During the 16th and 17th centuries, Portugal used Brazil as its primary source of sugar production, which was highly sought after in Europe. The cultivation of sugarcane on plantations was carried out by millions of enslaved Africans who worked under the harshest conditions, while profits were sent back to Portugal.

- **Gold:** By the end of the 17th century and throughout the 18th century, Brazil became the world's largest source of gold, with mines located in Minas Gerais and other interior regions of the country. This gold was crucial in sustaining Portugal, which faced financial struggles due to war expenditures in Europe. The Portuguese crown used Brazilian gold to finance wars and maintain its extravagant court. Wealth from Brazil was vital in keeping Portugal relevant on the international stage.

- **Enslavement:** The exploitation of humans as enslaved laborers was a core component of this system. According to some historical studies, over 4 million

Africans were brought to Brazil to work on plantations and in mines. While the Portuguese crown profited from the exploitation of the colonies, the enslaved workforce paid the highest price — a life of suffering, violence, and early death.

How Brazil's Wealth Sustained Portugal

Brazilian colonies saved Portugal from a prolonged financial crisis. During colonial dominance, Portugal relied almost entirely on Brazilian wealth to maintain its survival as an empire. Without sugar, gold, and other resources, Portugal would have been unable to retain its influence in Europe and would likely have been overtaken by other colonial powers, such as England or France.

The idea that Brazil was the "golden egg-laying hen" for Portugal is no exaggeration. During the gold cycle, the mines of Minas Gerais and Brazilian lands were the primary sources of wealth for the Portuguese crown, which did not hesitate to exploit every last economic potential of the colony.

2. BRAZILIAN EXPLOITATION AND POST-COLONIAL DISDAIN

While Portugal and Spain grew rich through resources and human exploitation in Brazil, after independence and the emancipation of former colonies, these same powers treated Brazilians with contempt, as if their contributions had never been vital to enriching the colonizing metropolises.

The Disrespectful Treatment of Brazilians

After independence, as colonial powers withdrew politically, the colonial mindset continued to shape international relations. Portugal, in particular, showed little recognition for Brazil's contribution to its wealth and prosperity, instead maintaining a policy of neglect and denial. During the Carnation Revolution in 1974, for example, Brazil was treated as a distant nation and often ignored in its internal struggles.

Portuguese historical references to Brazil often maintained a posture of superiority. This behavior reflects what many scholars refer to as **"structural racism"** and a colonial culture that extends into the present day, as seen in Portuguese attitudes toward Brazilians, who are frequently labeled as "exotic" or "inferior." The relationship between the two countries has always been marked by cultural discomfort and a significant emotional distance, particularly on Portugal's part, which frequently ignored Brazil's needs and voices.

3. THE LEGACY OF EXPLOITATION: CULTURAL AND ECONOMIC DEBT

Today, while Portugal and Spain still benefit from global trade and tourism networks, Brazil — which sustained these economies for centuries — remains a country with significant social and economic inequalities. The wealth extracted from Brazil sustained colonial powers, but Brazilians, particularly descendants of enslaved Africans and indigenous populations, face a harsh reality of poverty and marginalization.

- **The Legacy of Cultural Debt:** Brazil, as a young and emerging nation, carries the scars of colonial exploitation. The inheritance of racism, economic inequality, and regional disparities are just some of the consequences of this unequal relationship. While colonial powers like Portugal enriched themselves, Brazilian populations were forced to deal with dehumanization and the loss of cultural identity.

- **The Lack of Historical Reparations:** There has been no significant effort by colonizing nations to repair the wounds inflicted by colonialism. Although there is a growing global awareness of colonialism's consequences, Portugal's "debt" to Brazil remains unacknowledged, and reparations for the atrocities committed against indigenous and enslaved African populations remain an ignored issue.

4. FINAL REFLECTIONS

Brazil was crucial to the survival of the Portuguese empire, but this historical bond does not reflect the contemporary relationship between the two nations. The wealth extracted from Brazil largely financed Portugal's prosperity, while colonized populations lived under the weight of exploitation and oppression. Brazil today still bears the scars of this exploitation process that transformed a land rich in natural resources into a nation marked by social inequalities.

Portugal, despite benefiting enormously from Brazil, often denies the existence of a cultural and historical debt, ignoring the suffering of past generations and the need for genuine acknowledgment.

This chapter serves as a reminder that while capitalism built its foundation on the plundering of colonies, the impact of this system is still evident in the treatment of countries that once fed colonial powers with their wealth. The cultural and economic debt of colonialism remains, and the fight for justice and reparations continues to be a crucial issue in the relationship between these nations.

CHAPTER 10: MODERN CONFLICTS FUELED BY ECONOMIC INTERESTS

Global capitalism is not limited to causing damage in the past; its impacts strongly reverberate in the power dynamics and conflict policies of the contemporary world. Throughout history, wars and conflicts have often been, and continue to be, driven by economic interests. In the modern context, world powers and multinational corporations frequently act as the main agents that instigate and prolong conflicts, aiming to protect or expand their economic influence. This chapter explores how contemporary conflicts are shaped by these financial interests, political manipulation, and the relentless pursuit of profit, revealing the hidden face of war in the post-colonial world.

1. THE OIL WAR: THE ECONOMIC AXIS OF MIDDLE EASTERN CONFLICTS

The Middle East, a strategic region for oil supply, has become the epicenter of various modern conflicts, driven largely by economic interests as one of the primary driving forces. Oil is undoubtedly one of the world's most lucrative commodities, and the countries that control it, such as Saudi Arabia, Iraq, Iran, and others, are at the center of global disputes. Intervention in countries like Iraq and Syria, as well as power games in the Persian Gulf, illustrate how international economic interests are often the real reasons behind the conflicts that devastate the region.

- **The Iraq War (2003)**: Although justified as a response to Saddam Hussein's supposed arsenal of weapons of mass destruction, many analysts believe the true motivation was the control of Iraqi oil, one of the largest reserves in the world. The invasion of Iraq by a coalition led by the United States aimed to secure control over the country's oil wealth and strengthen access to Middle Eastern oil, a region essential for global energy supply. After the invasion, oil giants like Halliburton and Chevron were directly involved in reconstructing and exploiting Iraq's oil fields, highlighting the economic nature of the war.

- **The Role of Corporations**: Multinational corporations and the oil industry play a significant role in political decisions that lead to conflicts. Oil companies and their networks of influence in Western governments have been accused of manipulating and financing wars to secure lucrative contracts, access to natural resources, and new markets. These corporations act as a bridge between governments and private interests, creating a power dynamic where financial profit outweighs the lives affected by the conflict.

2. THE MILITARY-INDUSTRIAL COMPLEX: PROFITING FROM WAR

Another key driver of modern conflicts is the Military-Industrial Complex, a network of governments, military forces, and defense companies. Major defense corporations, such as Lockheed Martin, Boeing, Northrop Grumman, and Raytheon, sustain a war machine that not only profits from the production and supply of weapons but also benefits from the perpetuation of armed conflicts.

- **The Arms Trade**: The trade in weapons is one of the largest global markets, and often, the world's most powerful countries profit from selling military equipment to nations at war. America, for example, is one of the largest arms exporters globally, with billions of dollars in defense contracts annually. Economic interests are deeply intertwined with political decisions and military alliances.

- **War as a Business**: In a capitalist system, war has become an industry where destruction and suffering are converted into profit. The rise of armed conflicts, especially in the Middle East and Africa, often provides an opportunity for the Military-Industrial Complex to expand its business. Supplying weapons and military equipment is one of the most lucrative ways for these conglomerates to ensure survival and growth, relying on war to thrive. Instead of seeking peace, many of these interests prefer an unstable world where fear and violence drive demand for their goods.

3. THE ROLE OF NATURAL RESOURCES IN CONFLICTS

Many modern wars do not only focus on oil but also involve other essential natural resources, such as minerals, rare earths, precious metals, and water. The rampant exploitation of resources in developing countries often draws global powers into conflicts to secure control over these assets.

- **Africa and Mineral Conflicts**: The African continent, rich in minerals like diamonds, gold, coltan, and other precious metals, has been the site of civil wars and violent conflicts fueled largely by disputes over these resources. The illegal trade of minerals, such as "blood diamonds," has funded numerous wars in countries like Sierra Leone and the Democratic Republic of the Congo. Multinational corporations and global powers often purchase these resources at minimal prices, perpetuating suffering and conflicts in the region.

- **Amazon Exploitation and Territorial Conflicts**: The fight for control over the Amazon and other vital ecosystems is increasingly driven by economic interests. Deforestation for timber extraction, mining, and industrial agriculture has led to territorial conflicts with indigenous peoples and local communities, while governments and multinational companies seek unrestricted access to these natural resources.

4. GEOPOLITICS AND ECONOMIC INTERESTS IN REGIONAL WARS

In a connected and globalized world, economic powers seek to expand their spheres of influence and secure access to markets and essential natural resources. Civil and regional wars in places like Afghanistan, Syria, and Libya often stem from power disputes involving external interests. These wars are frequently fueled by foreign powers aiming to maintain or expand their influence in the region and control local resources.

- **Afghanistan**: Afghanistan, for instance, has been a crucial point in global geopolitics due to its strategic position and untapped natural resources. The war in Afghanistan, initially invaded by the United States in 2001, was motivated by factors including the presence of large lithium reserves, a mineral crucial for producing batteries and electronic devices. Additionally, the country's geographic position makes it vital for the global power strategy of major nations.

5. CONCLUSION: WAR AS AN INSTRUMENT OF ECONOMIC DOMINATION

Modern conflicts are often driven by economic interests that favor a small global elite at the expense of populations that pay the price with their lives. Oil, minerals, and the military-industrial complex are some of the primary forces behind these wars, while multinational corporations and global powers manipulate geopolitics to control resources and maintain the capitalist economic order. In a system where profit supersedes human well-being, war remains a powerful tool of exploitation, with devastating consequences for the affected populations. Capitalism, by sustaining these dynamics, exposes the true face of violence and destruction: the perpetuation of an economic system that thrives on the pain and suffering of others.

CHAPTER 11: HUMAN TRAFFICKING IN THE CAPITALIST ERA

Human trafficking is one of the darkest manifestations of exploitation within the capitalist system. Although slavery has been abolished in many parts of the world, a new form of slavery persists to this day—more hidden but equally devastating. Global capitalism, with its relentless focus on profit maximization and the exploitation of human vulnerabilities, is one of the main driving forces behind this heinous practice. Modern human trafficking involves the exploitation of men, women, and children for forced labor, sexual exploitation, and other forms of contemporary slavery. This chapter will explore how capitalism, with its economic dynamics, consumer systems, and corporate practices, fuels and perpetuates human trafficking, revealing how this industry of pain and suffering is deeply entwined with the functioning of the global market.

1. HUMAN TRAFFICKING AS A PROFITABLE INDUSTRY

Human trafficking is a multi-billion-dollar industry fueled by the insatiable demand for cheap labor and the exploitation of human bodies for sexual or forced labor purposes. Capitalism, at its core, relies on an available workforce, which, in many cases, is vulnerable and exploitable. Human trafficking is a direct extension of this capitalist logic, where the need for profit and the pursuit of maximum exploitation create a black market for slave labor.

- **The Labor Market and the Pursuit of Cheap Labor:** In capitalist countries, where the consumer system demands constant and limitless production, cheap labor becomes a valuable resource. Many products consumed by wealthy countries are, in fact, produced by workers under extremely precarious conditions or even in situations resembling modern-day slavery. Human trafficking serves as a tool to supply this dirty labor market, where the exploitation of human lives is not only tolerated but encouraged to reduce production costs and increase profits for multinational companies.

- **The Sex Industry and Sexual Exploitation:** Human trafficking is also closely linked to sexual exploitation. Women and children, in particular, are trafficked into prostitution networks and sexual exploitation around the world. Capitalism, with its relentless pursuit of satisfying desires and consumption, creates an environment where the sexualization and objectification of individuals become currency. In many cases, human trafficking is a direct response to the demand for cheap and readily available sexual services, often fueled by a consumerist and dehumanizing society.

2. THE CONNECTION WITH MULTINATIONAL CORPORATIONS

Human trafficking is not an isolated practice confined to underground markets. It is intertwined with the practices of large multinational corporations that, often unknowingly or, in some cases, directly, benefit from this illegal trade. Capitalist globalization, which promotes a borderless market and economic interdependence between countries, facilitates human trafficking, making it a global issue that involves a vast network of corporations, governments, and other institutions.

- **Forced Labor in Supply Chains:** Many multinational companies, especially in the clothing, electronics, mining, and agriculture industries, rely on cheap labor that is often exploited. Southeast Asian, African, and Latin American workers are frequently trafficked to work in factories, mines, and plantations that supply products for major brands. Factories producing clothing for brands like Nike, Adidas, and other industry giants have been linked to forced labor, often driven by human trafficking networks. Although companies claim to take measures against these practices, the profit generated by exploitation remains the primary motivation for maintaining these production systems.

- **Sex Tourism and Major Corporations:** Sex tourism is one of the darkest areas of human trafficking, with large tourism companies and travel agencies operating in markets where the sexual exploitation of children and adults is a profitable business. The supply chains for the tourism industry can also be connected to human trafficking, as some travel agencies and tourism operators may, consciously or unconsciously, facilitate the transportation of victims to locations where prostitution and sexual exploitation are rampant.

3. THE LACK OF REGULATION AND THE GLOBAL TRAFFICKING INDUSTRY

The lack of regulation and oversight of human trafficking networks is a direct result of governments' unwillingness to address the depths of exploitation that capitalism generates. In many countries, especially those in developing regions, public policies are insufficient to combat human trafficking effectively, and corruption within government spheres further fuels this illicit market.

- **Corruption and Government Exploitation:** Often, human trafficking is facilitated by corruption in local or national governments, which allow these networks to operate with minimal interference. In countries where poverty is extreme and job opportunities are limited, the exploitation of vulnerable populations becomes a profitable practice for both traffickers and corrupt governments that receive bribes to turn a blind eye or even collaborate with trafficking networks.

- **The Role of Corporations in Low-Regulation Countries:** In countries with weak legislation, such as many nations in Africa, Asia, and Latin America, multinational corporations can operate with little to no control, creating a perfect environment for worker exploitation and the perpetuation of human trafficking. Laws prohibiting forced labor and sexual exploitation are often ineffective, and human trafficking networks take advantage of these shortcomings to ensure a continuous flow of victims to the market.

4. THE INTERNATIONAL RESPONSE TO HUMAN TRAFFICKING

Although the international community has adopted measures to combat human trafficking, such as the Palermo Protocol, which aims to prevent, suppress, and punish human trafficking, the implementation of these policies is inconsistent and often ineffective. International organizations, such as the UN, have made significant efforts to eradicate human trafficking, but political unwillingness, corruption, and impunity remain key obstacles.

- **Corporate Social Responsibility Initiatives:** Some companies and organizations have worked to improve transparency in their supply chains by implementing stricter policies against forced labor. However, these initiatives are often superficial and fail to address the fundamental issue of an economic system that relies on the exploitation of human labor to thrive.

- **The Fight Against Trafficking: The Role of NGOs and Social Movements:** Non-governmental organizations and social movements play a crucial role in rescuing and supporting victims of human trafficking. However, these organizations often face significant challenges due to a lack of funding, political support, and the complexity of global trafficking networks.

5. CONCLUSION: CAPITALISM AS THE ENGINE OF HUMAN TRAFFICKING

Modern human trafficking is a direct expression of global capitalism in its most ruthless form. It is fueled by the relentless pursuit of profit, the exploitation of human vulnerabilities, and the lack of effective market regulation. Human trafficking, whether for forced labor or sexual exploitation, remains a profitable practice that involves multinational corporations, corrupt governments, and an international network of traffickers. In a system that prioritizes profit over human well-being, human trafficking becomes a parallel but essential industry for the survival and growth of capitalism. Combating this practice requires a radical transformation of the global economic system, one that prioritizes human dignity and social justice over exploitation and modern-day slavery.

CHAPTER 12: CONTEMPORARY SLAVE LABOR AND SEXUAL EXPLOITATION

Contemporary slave labor and sexual exploitation are, unfortunately, among the most visible and devastating practices within the global capitalist economy. In a system that prioritizes profit over human dignity, people are treated as commodities, forced to work in inhumane conditions, or exploited for sexual purposes. This chapter explores how capitalism fuels these practices, with a focus on the "fast fashion" industry and its connections to child labor and sexual exploitation.

1. CONTEMPORARY SLAVE LABOR IN GLOBAL CAPITALISM

Modern slave labor, also known as "contemporary slavery," is a grim reality affecting millions of people worldwide. In many countries, especially in the most impoverished regions, people are forced to work in extreme exploitation, without fair wages or rights. This system of exploitation is driven by economic interests that seek to maximize profits while minimizing production costs. Modern slave labor can be found in various industries, such as agriculture, mining, construction, and more recently, in the production of goods for the global market.

- **High-Profit, Low-Cost Industries:** Many industries, such as agriculture, mining, and clothing production, rely on forced labor as a way to reduce production costs. Capitalism, with its relentless need to maximize profits, makes these practices acceptable within the global economic system. In countries where labor oversight is weak or nonexistent, traffickers and unscrupulous employers exploit vulnerable workers, many of whom are enslaved in conditions akin to slavery.

- **Many Workers Are Invisible:** Contemporary slave labor is often invisible to the end consumer, who buys products without knowing what lies behind their production. Clothing factories, coffee plantations, diamond mines, and other products are often associated with forced labor, where victims, frequently women and children, are deprived of their freedom, forced to live in degrading conditions, and work long hours without adequate compensation.

2. SEXUAL EXPLOITATION IN GLOBAL CAPITALISM

Sexual exploitation, particularly of women and children, has deep roots in global capitalism. The sex industry, driven by the demand for cheap services and the objectification of human bodies, thrives in a system where profit is prioritized over dignity and well-being. Like slave labor, sexual exploitation is not just a byproduct of capitalism but an integral part of the global economy.

- **Prostitution and Sex Tourism:** Sex tourism is a growing phenomenon, especially in countries with weak or developing economies, where women and children are often trafficked for sexual exploitation. Large tourism and travel companies often do not care about the ultimate fate of their customers and, in some cases, are even inadvertently or unregulated accomplices in facilitating this exploitation. Capitalism, in its relentless pursuit of pleasure and consumption, creates a market where sex and the sexual exploitation of minors become commodities.

- **Sex Trafficking and the Consumer Market:** The sex trafficking industry is a significant part of the global economy of sexual exploitation. Women and girls are often kidnapped or deceived with promises of jobs, only to find themselves forced to work as prostitutes or in other sexual services. Many of these victims are left without resources and support, making them dependent on their traffickers and clients, who often pay a fraction of the value that these victims would earn if they had any form of compensation.

3. The "Fast Fashion" Industry and Its Connections to

Child Labor

The "fast fashion" industry exemplifies the direct connection between capitalism, contemporary slave labor, and child exploitation. Fast fashion refers to the mass production of cheap clothing that quickly reaches retail stores, driven by the demand for new trends at affordable prices. This business model relies on a supply chain that maximizes profits but puts workers' lives at risk, particularly in the world's most impoverished regions.

- **The Role of Child Labor in Fast Fashion:** To produce cheap clothing, many major fast fashion brands have factories located in countries with weak or nonexistent labor laws. In these countries, children are employed in clothing factories, often in dangerous and unhealthy conditions, to sew, pack, and process products sold in large retail chains. Child labor, fueled by the exploitation of vulnerable families that need money to survive, is a common practice in many of these factories.

- **Exploitative Supply Chains:** Fast fashion relies on complex and often opaque global supply chains involving factories and suppliers in countries like Bangladesh, India, Pakistan, and others. These factories, frequently exposed for conditions akin to slavery, offer meager wages and demand long working hours from employees, including children. Many of these multinational companies either know or should know the conditions under which their products are made but continue to benefit from low production costs, allowing child labor and slave-like conditions to remain part of their business structure.

- **Sexual Exploitation in Clothing Factories:** In some cases, sexual exploitation is also present in fast fashion factories. Women and girls, often vulnerable and without resources, are coerced into working in factories only to be subjected to sexual abuse to retain their jobs or receive a paycheck. Factories employing these workers frequently disregard human rights and maintain victims in vulnerable conditions, making them more susceptible to abuse.

4. SOCIAL AND CULTURAL CONSEQUENCES OF EXPLOITATION

The exploitation of workers in fast fashion and sexual exploitation has devastating consequences not only for the victims but also for society as a whole. The normalization of exploitation and human suffering in pursuit of profit has a profound impact on communities and cultures.

- **Normalization of Exploitation:** Global capitalism normalizes the idea that the exploitation of human bodies is acceptable to generate profit. In many parts of the world, especially in communities where child labor is common, exploitation becomes a social norm. Children and women, whose voices are often silenced, become invisible cogs in the machinery of the global industry.

- **Psychological Impacts:** Victims of modern slave labor and sexual exploitation face severe psychological consequences. Many of these people live with trauma, constant fear, and a loss of identity and dignity. For women and children trafficked and forced into prostitution or slave labor in factories, daily life becomes a nightmare of abuse, suffering, and degradation.

5. CONCLUSION: THE FIGHT AGAINST SLAVE LABOR AND SEXUAL EXPLOITATION IN CAPITALISM

Modern slave labor and sexual exploitation are integral and invisible parts of the capitalist system. Major fast fashion and sex tourism industries drive these markets, while large corporations and governments often perpetuate the cycle of abuse and exploitation. To effectively combat these practices, a global movement is needed to challenge the power structures that allow human exploitation to remain a profitable practice. This requires not only awareness about the impacts of capitalism on the lives of millions but also concrete action to change the economic structures that perpetuate human suffering.

CHAPTER 13: MASSACRES FOR PROFIT

CAPITALISM, IN ITS RELENTLESS PURSUIT OF PROFIT, OFTEN SACRIFICES HUMAN LIVES IN THE NAME OF EFFICIENCY AND COST REDUCTION. MASSACRES DRIVEN BY LARGE CORPORATIONS AND ECONOMIC INTERESTS HAVE BEEN SEEN THROUGHOUT HISTORY, WHERE COMPANIES PRIORITIZE PROFITS OVER THE SAFETY, HEALTH, AND DIGNITY OF INDIVIDUALS. THIS CHAPTER FOCUSES ON SOME OF THE MOST DEVASTATING TRAGEDIES CAUSED BY GREED, WITH AN IN-DEPTH LOOK AT THE BHOPAL DISASTER IN INDIA AND OTHER EXAMPLES OF INDUSTRIAL MASSACRES.

1. The Bhopal Disaster: The Largest Industrial Accident in History

The Bhopal disaster, which occurred in 1984, stands as one of the most infamous industrial tragedies in modern history and a glaring testament to how capitalism can put human lives at risk in the name of profit. The accident took place in the city of Bhopal in central India at the Union Carbide India Limited (UCIL) plant, a subsidiary of the American giant Union Carbide Corporation (UCC). A toxic gas leak (methyl isocyanate) resulted in the deaths of thousands of people and exposed hundreds of thousands to severe poisoning.

- **Causes of the Disaster:** The gas leak was the direct result of negligence and cost-cutting measures. The factory was poorly maintained and operated with defective equipment. The lack of maintenance, combined with the decision to reduce the number of employees and the budget allocated to safety, created a scenario ripe for disaster. The company, aiming to maximize profits, sacrificed the safety of workers and surrounding communities, exposing them to mortal danger.

- **Human Impact:** The exact number of victims was never determined, but estimates suggest that between 3,000 and 8,000 people died in the weeks following the gas leak, with around 500,000 people suffering from long-term health issues, such as respiratory diseases, vision problems, and psychological disorders. Children born after the disaster also showed congenital defects and health problems due to exposure to the toxic gas.

- **The Role of Corporations:** Union Carbide's response is a classic example of how large corporations minimize the consequences of their actions in the pursuit of profit. The company initially tried to deflect responsibility for the disaster, claiming it was caused by sabotage, without admitting its negligence. Furthermore, the compensation offered to victims was minimal compared to the damage caused. Justice for the Bhopal victims was delayed for decades, and although the company was sued, those responsible were never properly punished.

2. THE MINAMATA TRAGEDY: MERCURY AND THE LUCRATIVE DISREGARD FOR HUMAN LIFE

Another example of an industrial massacre with roots in capitalism is the Minamata case in Japan, where mercury was indiscriminately dumped into the water system, leading to a series of severe poisoning incidents in the 1950s. The Chisso Corporation, a major chemical company, was mainly responsible for the disaster by discharging mercury waste into Minamata Bay, contaminating local fish and water. Thousands of people, including fishermen and their families, suffered from the effects of mercury poisoning, a neurological disease known as "Minamata disease."

- **Corporate Negligence and Profit Pursuit:** Chisso not only ignored environmental safety standards but also covered up the extent of the disaster for years, continuing to operate the factory while thousands of lives were devastated. The company prioritized maximizing profits and maintained its negligence for economic reasons, failing to implement necessary changes to prevent contamination.

- **Human Consequences:** Minamata disease severely affected victims, causing irreversible neurological damage, deformities, and death. Affected families fought for decades to obtain compensation and recognition, while Chisso attempted to minimize its responsibility.

3. ENVIRONMENTAL EXPLOITATION AND THE RANA PLAZA CATASTROPHE

The Rana Plaza tragedy in 2013 provides further evidence of how capitalism, in its quest for profits at any cost, can result in death and destruction. The collapse of the Rana Plaza building in Bangladesh, which housed factories for global clothing brands, led to the deaths of over 1,100 workers and left thousands more severely injured. The building, already showing visible cracks, remained operational due to pressure from companies to meet "fast fashion" demands.

- **Profit Pursuit at the Cost of Human Life:** Rana Plaza symbolized how major clothing brands push for mass production at extremely low prices. Workers, mostly women and children, were forced to work long hours in unsafe conditions with wages below the minimum. The building collapse was a foreseeable tragedy, but the companies involved, which profited from the exploitation, were largely spared from consequences.

- **Corporate Responsibility:** Although victims and their families fought for justice, major "fast fashion" brands that benefited from exploiting Bangladeshi workers were rarely held adequately accountable. Global capitalism, in its relentless pursuit of cheap profits, encouraged this kind of neglect and disregard for human life, with justice remaining slow and insufficient.

4. ENVIRONMENTAL DISASTERS CAUSED BY CORPORATE GREED

In addition to industrial tragedies, capitalism is also responsible for a series of environmental disasters that have led to the deaths of thousands of people and the devastation of entire ecosystems. The 2010 Gulf of Mexico oil spill, caused by BP, is a prime example of how corporations, in search of profits, ignore environmental risks and endanger human lives and the environment.

- **The Chernobyl Disaster:** Although not directly caused by private corporations, the Chernobyl nuclear accident in 1986 is an example of how centralized and corrupt economic systems, like the Soviet regime, can neglect safety and cause tragedies in the name of economic development. The disaster resulted in the deaths of dozens of people and affected the health of hundreds of thousands of others.

- **Environmental Impact of Capitalism:** By prioritizing profit maximization over human and environmental well-being, capitalism creates a continuous cycle of destruction and exploitation. Environmental disasters are often minimized or ignored by governments and corporations, and victims, usually the most vulnerable, face prolonged legal battles to seek justice.

5. CONCLUSION: THE PRICE OF PROFIT

The tragedies discussed in this chapter are just some of the many examples showing that capitalism, in its insatiable pursuit of profit, can lead to death, suffering, and destruction. Companies and governments that prioritize profit over safety, health, and well-being not only disrespect human life but also perpetuate a system that places economic interests above everything else, including morality. To prevent future massacres and disasters, it is necessary to rethink the global economic system and seek ways to produce and consume that respect life, human rights, and the environment.

CHAPTER 14: GENOCIDES FUNDED BY CORPORATE INTERESTS

Corporate interests are often the driving forces behind genocides, not only through direct economic exploitation but also through forms of abuse that involve the marginalization, destruction, and even eradication of entire populations to pave the way for profits. This chapter examines how corporations, driven by the need to expand their markets and exploit natural resources, have funded and sustained genocides throughout history, with a particular focus on mining operations and their devastating impact on indigenous peoples.

1. THE CORPORATE ROLE IN COLONIAL GENOCIDES

During the colonial period, European powers, with the support of large corporations, were responsible for a series of genocides, where indigenous populations were subjected to brutal and systematic exploitation in search of natural resources. The corporations involved, with their financial and political power, were crucial in maintaining massacres in various parts of the world, where entire populations were either exterminated or forced into servitude.

- **Example: The Herero and Namaqua Genocide (1904-1908)**
  At the beginning of the 20th century, Germany, through its corporations like the Deutsche Kolonialgesellschaft, was involved in a systematic genocide against the Herero and Namaqua peoples in present-day Namibia. Germany sought to expand its control over the region's diamond and other natural resources. The extermination of around 100,000 people, or approximately 80% of the Herero population, was justified by the desire to control lucrative resources, supported by companies that directly benefited from forced labor.

- **Gold Exploration and the Invasion of Indigenous Peoples in the Amazon**
  Throughout the 19th and 20th centuries, corporate interest in the vast gold and mineral reserves of the Amazon intensified, leading to the destruction of indigenous communities and the silent genocide of populations forced to abandon their lands. Mining companies seeking to expand operations frequently

financed and allied with corrupt governments to access natural riches, often resulting in violence, forced displacement, and even mass deaths. The *"Gold War"*, fought in Brazil during the gold cycle and more recently in contemporary times, is an example of how corporate interests can lead to genocides.

2. MINING OPERATIONS AND THE IMPACT ON INDIGENOUS PEOPLES

The extraction of natural resources, particularly minerals, has been a primary cause of violent conflicts and genocides. Often, the interest of large corporations and governments in controlling mines and lands rich in resources results in the displacement and destruction of indigenous cultures. Mining, one of the most profitable sectors in the global economy, has been responsible for some of the most brutal forms of exploitation and violence against indigenous peoples.

- **The Cobalt Mines in Congo (Democratic Republic of the Congo)**
  Cobalt mining, a mineral essential for producing electric vehicle batteries and electronics, is largely controlled by multinational corporations. The Democratic Republic of the Congo, rich in cobalt, has experienced intense exploitation, with indigenous populations forced to work under inhuman conditions, without any rights. The Congolese government, in alliance with foreign corporations, has tolerated abuse in the name of profit, with intensive exploitation of children and adult workers in mines. Many of these individuals live in near-slavery conditions while companies reap massive profits.

- **Gold and Diamond Exploitation in Brazil**
  Brazil, with its vast reserves of gold and diamonds, has also seen severe violations against indigenous peoples. In regions like the Amazon, mining companies have invaded indigenous lands, destroying forests and exposing local communities to diseases, contamination, and direct violence. The case of illegal

mining operations on Yanomami territory resulted in disease epidemics and even massacres. These companies, supported by a web of political and corporate interests, continue to exploit these lands, disregarding indigenous communities' legitimate claims.

3. OIL EXPLORATION AND THE IMPACT ON INDIGENOUS PEOPLES

Apart from mining, the oil industry is another sector that has generated genocides funded by corporate interests. Major oil companies, in partnership with governments, have caused environmental and human destruction in various regions around the world, affecting indigenous communities that rely on the land for their survival.

- **The Devastation of Indigenous Peoples in the Amazon**

  The Amazon, with its vast oil and gas reserves, has been a constant target for major oil corporations. The impact on indigenous peoples in the region is catastrophic. Companies like Chevron and Petrobras have been responsible for oil spills, water pollution, and the destruction of ecosystems crucial to indigenous communities. Oil exploration on indigenous lands, such as the cases of the Kayapo and Xingu peoples, has led to violent confrontations, deaths, and the dismantling of their cultures.

- **Example: Shell in the Niger Delta**

  In the Niger Delta, oil exploration by Shell resulted in an environmental and social massacre of immense proportions. Indigenous peoples like the Ogoni were forced to live in highly contaminated environments, with their lands devastated in the name of profit. In 1995, after years of peaceful resistance, the Nigerian government, in collaboration with Shell, executed nine Ogoni leaders in a brutal crackdown on the movement that opposed oil exploration on their lands. This event marked one of the most brutal corporate-sponsored genocides driven by natural resource exploitation.

4. MODERN GENOCIDES: NATURAL RESOURCE EXPLOITATION AND INDIGENOUS MASSACRES

In the 21st century, the exploitation of natural resources in regions with large indigenous populations continues to be a source of genocides and massacres. Major corporations remain the main entities funding violence against indigenous peoples, often with the support of corrupt governments that profit from extractive activities.

- **The Case of Guatemala and Silver Mining**
  In Guatemala, silver mining has had severe impacts on indigenous communities. Mining corporations, often tied to local political interests, exploit these populations, disregarding their rights and territorial protection. In 2010, violent repression against the indigenous Xinca people protesting the construction of a silver mine resulted in massacres and torture. Mining companies continue to operate in these regions while victims face the loss of their lands, resources, and lives.

- **Amazon Deforestation and Indigenous Peoples**
  The ongoing deforestation of the Amazon, driven by demand for land for mining, agriculture, and timber production, has led to large-scale genocides against indigenous communities. The Brazilian government, in collaboration with major multinational companies, has encouraged the unchecked exploitation of natural resources in the region, often ignoring laws that protect indigenous lands. As a result, peoples like the Kayapo, Munduruku, and Yanomami face constant threats of extermination, while corporations profit

from the destruction of their territories.

5. CONCLUSION: CAPITALISM AND THE GENOCIDE OF INDIGENOUS PEOPLES

Capitalism, with its relentless pursuit of profit, continues to be a driving force of destruction and genocide. The exploitation of mines and natural resources, often supported by large corporations, has caused the suffering and elimination of indigenous peoples in various parts of the world. These genocides are not only a reflection of exploitative policies but also of the systematic disregard for human rights and the dignity of native populations. To break this cycle of violence, it is necessary to reform capitalism in a way that protects indigenous peoples and ensures that economic interests do not come before social and environmental responsibility.

CHAPTER 15: GLOBAL INEQUALITY — HOW CAPITALISM PERPETUATES INEQUALITY

Capitalism, as the dominant economic system in the world, is often seen as the primary force driving global inequality. Although it has been promoted as a model that ensures economic freedom, individual prosperity, and growth, in practice, capitalism has consolidated disparities in wealth and power, deepening the divide between the privileged few and the impoverished masses. This chapter will analyze how capitalism perpetuates and exacerbates inequality, affecting different regions of the world, from developed countries to the poorest and most vulnerable nations.

1. THE CYCLE OF WEALTH AND POVERTY: CAPITALISM AS A MECHANISM FOR WEALTH ACCUMULATION

The fundamental principle of capitalism is capital accumulation through the exploitation of natural resources, labor, and global markets. The profits generated by this process are largely concentrated in the hands of a small elite, while the majority of the global population lives in poverty or underdeveloped conditions. Economic inequality, in both developed and developing countries, is a reflection of how capitalism disproportionately distributes the wealth generated.

- **Example: Wealth Concentration in the USA and Growing Inequality**
  In the United States, the concentration of wealth in the hands of a few billionaires, such as Jeff Bezos, Elon Musk, and Bill Gates, is a clear example of how capitalism fosters inequality. In 2023, the wealthiest 1% of the U.S. population owned over 30% of the national wealth, while the bottom 50% owned less than 2% of it. This growing chasm between rich and poor is a central feature of modern capitalism, where the system benefits capital owners, while workers and lower classes are left at the mercy of a market that offers no security or mobility opportunities.

2. LABOR EXPLOITATION: THE SOURCE OF INEQUALITY IN CAPITALISM

The primary source of wealth in capitalism is labor, but this labor is rarely rewarded fairly. The exploitation of the workforce, in both developed and developing countries, is one of the main ways capitalism perpetuates inequality. Large corporations that dominate global markets aim to minimize labor costs by paying low wages and offering poor working conditions, especially in Third World countries.

- **Example: The Technology Industry and Precarious Work**

  Companies like Amazon, Apple, and Google are known for their labor exploitation practices, both in distribution centers and factories supplied by partners like Foxconn in China. Workers face precarious conditions, long hours, and low pay, while corporate elites accumulate billion-dollar fortunes. This contributes to an enormous wealth disparity, with a small elite capitalizing on the work of millions of low-cost laborers.

- **Example: The Fashion Industry and Global Labor Exploitation**

  Capitalism also perpetuates global inequality in the fashion industry, where luxury brands and major retailers, such as Nike and H&M, benefit from child labor and the exploitation of workers in factories in Southeast Asia and Africa. The relentless pursuit of low profits costs lives and human rights, while major brands maintain astronomical profits. Factory work in the clothing industry is one of the most visible forms of exploitation in capitalism, with an alarming number of workers, mostly women and children, living in degrading conditions.

3. THE CAPITALIST EMPIRE: INEQUALITY BETWEEN DEVELOPED AND DEVELOPING COUNTRIES

One of the most evident ways capitalism perpetuates inequality is through the unequal relationships between developed and developing countries. The global capitalist system has been structured to exploit the natural resources and labor of poorer nations while rich economies benefit from this exploitation.

- **Example: Colonization and its Lasting Effects**
  The colonial era and imperialism established an economic exploitation system where colonizing countries, such as the UK, France, Portugal, and Spain, looted natural resources from colonies in Africa, Asia, and Latin America. This exploitation not only enriched colonial powers but also established an economic inequality pattern that persists to this day. The wealth extracted from these regions, such as gold, spices, coffee, sugar, and oil, helped finance the development of colonizing nations, while colonized populations were impoverished and marginalized.

- **Example: The Global Division of Labor and Resource Exploitation**
  Global capitalism has maintained a system where countries in the Global South provide natural resources and raw materials to the economies of the Global North, without seeing significant benefits. Countries like South Africa, Brazil, and other Latin American nations export minerals and agricultural goods, but the majority of their populations remain in extreme poverty, while multinational corporations in wealthy countries accumulate substantial profits.

4. EXTERNAL DEBT AND THE CYCLE OF DEPENDENCY

Another mechanism through which capitalism perpetuates global inequality is through the external debt imposed on developing countries. International banks, such as the IMF (International Monetary Fund) and the World Bank, lend large sums of money to developing nations, often at high-interest rates. These loans, often used to finance infrastructure or military projects, end up creating unsustainable debt cycles that result in greater poverty for these nations.

- **Example: The Latin American Debt Crisis**
  During the 1970s and 1980s, many Latin American countries, including Mexico, Brazil, and Argentina, incurred massive external debts with international financial institutions. These loans were used to finance development and modernization projects, but instead of benefiting local populations, they led to increased poverty and inequality, as resources were diverted to debt service and the interests of local and international elites. To this day, Latin America remains one of the most indebted regions in the world, with many countries struggling to stabilize their economies.

5. INEQUALITY IN THE GLOBAL TRADE SYSTEM

The international trade system, dominated by agreements such as the World Trade Organization (WTO), favors developed economies while marginalizing developing economies. The rules of global trade, with unequal tariffs and agricultural subsidies provided by rich countries, keep developing nations dependent and without access to fair markets.

- **Example: The Agricultural Industry and Rich Country Subsidies**

  In the United States and the European Union, the agricultural subsidy system benefits large producers and maintains artificially low commodity prices. This undermines farmers in developing countries, who cannot compete fairly in international markets. As a result, millions of farmers in poor countries face a constant struggle for survival, while agricultural corporations in rich countries continue to thrive.

6. CONCLUSION: CAPITALISM'S PERPETUATION OF GLOBAL INEQUALITY

Throughout history, capitalism has been an economic system that promotes and perpetuates global inequality. From labor exploitation to the plundering of natural resources and the imposition of external debt, capitalism concentrates wealth and power in a small global elite, while the masses continue to live in poverty. To change this reality, a profound rethinking of the global economic system is necessary, with a focus on social justice, wealth redistribution, and reparations for historical injustices. Inequality is not an inevitable consequence but a choice resulting from the policies and practices of capitalism.

CHAPTER 17: THE IMPACT OF NEOLIBERAL ECONOMY

Neoliberalism, as an economic model, emerged as a reaction against the welfare state and interventionist economic systems that prevailed after World War II. Rooted in the theories of economists like Milton Friedman and Friedrich Hayek, neoliberalism advocates for a reduction in state intervention in the economy, trade liberalization, and the deregulation of markets. The central premise of neoliberalism is that free markets, free from state controls, would be the most efficient in generating wealth, benefiting society as a whole, and driving economic growth. However, over the past few decades, neoliberalism has demonstrated devastating effects on society, resulting in greater wealth concentration, increased inequalities, and deteriorating living conditions for a large part of the population.

THE RISE OF NEOLIBERALISM

Neoliberalism gained prominence in the 1980s, particularly with the rise of leaders like Ronald Reagan in the United States and Margaret Thatcher in the United Kingdom. Both implemented policies of privatization, tax cuts for the wealthy, deregulation of industries, and the reduction of social programs. These governments, along with institutions like the International Monetary Fund (IMF) and the World Bank, began to impose neoliberal reforms in developing countries by offering loans in exchange for structural adjustment packages. These packages included severe economic measures such as public spending cuts and the privatization of essential resources.

PRIVATIZATION AND CUTS TO SOCIAL RIGHTS

One of the key characteristics of neoliberalism is the privatization of public services and the sale of state assets. From energy and water sectors to education and healthcare, services that were once considered fundamental rights began to be treated as commodities. Private companies, often multinational corporations, took control of these services, prioritizing profit over social welfare. As a result, access to essential services like quality healthcare and education decreased, creating greater social inequalities.

Additionally, neoliberalism led to cuts in social welfare programs, such as pensions, unemployment benefits, and social assistance programs. In countries like Brazil, for instance, the implementation of neoliberal policies reduced the state's role in social protection, negatively affecting the most vulnerable segments of the population.

WEALTH CONCENTRATION AND INCREASED INEQUALITIES

Instead of shared prosperity, as neoliberalism promised, historical data shows that neoliberal policies resulted in wealth concentration among a small elite. The reduction of taxes on large corporations and the wealthy, coupled with deregulated financial markets, allowed big companies and individuals to accumulate fortunes, while workers' incomes stagnated or decreased. The rise of job insecurity, with the growth of informal employment and underemployment, further deepened social inequalities.

Globally, neoliberalism also had a devastating impact on developing countries. The IMF and World Bank's "structural adjustment" policies resulted in financial crises, increased external debt, and economic hardships for millions of people. Many of these countries, unable to repay their debts, saw their economies weakened, losing sovereignty and experiencing intensified exploitation of natural resources by foreign corporations.

THE ENVIRONMENTAL IMPACT OF NEOLIBERALISM

Another devastating effect of neoliberal policies is the environmental impact. With deregulation and an emphasis on profit above all else, the rampant exploitation of natural resources—such as timber, oil, and minerals—increased significantly. Industries, often operating without proper oversight, contributed to deforestation, pollution, and the depletion of natural resources in many parts of the world.

In the case of the Amazon, for example, the advance of neoliberalism led to increased deforestation to make way for soybean plantations and cattle ranching, driven by multinational companies that benefited from the lack of environmental regulation. This had catastrophic consequences not only for local communities but also for global climate balance, as the Amazon plays a crucial role in regulating the Earth's climate.

THE PRECARIOUSNESS OF WORK AND THE FLEXIBILITY OF LABOR LAWS

Neoliberalism also imposed labor law flexibility, allowing for more precarious working conditions with fewer protections for workers. "Flexibility" often meant reducing labor rights, such as paid vacations, a 13th salary, dignified retirement, and unemployment insurance. The increase in outsourcing and temporary jobs also meant less job stability and security, particularly affecting lower classes.

THE 2008 FINANCIAL CRISIS AND THE COLLAPSE OF NEOLIBERALISM

The global financial crisis of 2008 dramatically exposed the flaws of the neoliberal model. The collapse of financial markets, caused by unregulated speculative practices and the devaluation of real estate assets, resulted in a worldwide recession, affecting millions of people around the globe. Neoliberal policies of deregulation and tax cuts for the wealthy did not prevent the crisis but rather exacerbated it, showing that markets, without intervention, were incapable of correcting their own failures.

Despite this, many of the world's most powerful countries continued to adopt neoliberal policies, prioritizing the interests of large corporations and privatization of essential services. Even after the crisis, austerity measures were imposed on countries like Greece, Portugal, and Spain, leading to worsened living conditions for working-class populations and perpetuating inequality.

THE LEGACY OF NEOLIBERALISM

Neoliberalism left a legacy of social inequality, exploitation, and deregulation, and continues to be a dominant system in many countries. Its effects are evident in growing income disparities, weakened social safety nets, environmental degradation, and the intensification of exploitation among the working class.

Despite the criticism and economic crises that arose from its failures, neoliberalism continues to shape policies worldwide, perpetuating a global economy where profitability is prioritized over human and environmental well-being.

CHAPTER 18: ECONOMIC CRISES AND THEIR VICTIMS

Economic crises are mostly the result of failures within capitalist systems that seek to maximize profit and minimize costs, often at the expense of social well-being. As we will see, these crises not only affect financial markets and companies but also have a devastating impact on working classes and the most vulnerable in society. The exploitation and deregulation that characterize capitalism frequently lead to these economic breakdowns, which further accentuate inequalities and deepen poverty.

THE 1929 COLLAPSE AND ITS CONSEQUENCES

The 1929 Crash, also known as the Great Depression, was one of the most devastating economic crises in modern history. This collapse originated in the United States and quickly spread worldwide, destroying economies and plunging millions into poverty. The New York stock market, driven by rampant speculation, collapsed as investors began selling their stocks in mass, leading to a loss of confidence in markets and a domino effect that affected the entire global economy.

The 1929 crisis exposed the fundamental flaws of an unregulated capitalism: the relentless pursuit of profit, without proper controls, led to overproduction, speculation, and financial bubbles. When these bubbles burst, the consequences were catastrophic for the population. Millions lost their jobs, their homes, and their savings. Factories closed, trade paralyzed, and hunger and poverty spread. In a country like the United States, which prided itself as the "land of opportunity," poverty was visible everywhere. Entire families were forced to live in makeshift tents, while the wealthy who caused the crisis continued to maintain their fortunes.

In Latin America, the crisis deepened as countries relied on exports of products such as coffee, minerals, and sugar to Europe and the United States. With the collapse of global trade, these countries saw their economies crumble, resulting in waves of political and social instability. Poverty spread on an unprecedented scale.

MODERN FINANCIAL CRISES AND THE GENERATED POVERTY

The 1929 crisis was not an isolated phenomenon. Capitalism, with its relentless pursuit of profit and reliance on volatile financial markets, continues to generate cyclical economic crises that particularly affect the poorest. The 2008 financial collapse is a clear example of how failures within the financial system, fueled by excessive speculation and a lack of proper regulation, have devastating impacts on vulnerable populations.

The 2008 Global Financial Crisis, originating from the bankruptcy of major banks in the United States overloaded with debt and risky investments, spread quickly worldwide with destruction. The global banking system collapsed, leading to a series of bankruptcies, mass layoffs, and a global recession. Poverty increased dramatically, especially in countries where people already lived on low wages and in precarious jobs. The labor market was saturated with low-paying jobs, and millions of families lost their homes, while large banking corporations were bailed out by the government with billions of dollars in rescue packages.

In developing countries, the crisis had an even more devastating effect. The decline in demand for exported goods, the strength of the dollar, and the drop in commodity prices led to a sharp decrease in local economies, deeply affecting the poor. At the same time, neoliberal austerity policies implemented by institutions like the IMF and World Bank required cuts in essential social services, such as health, education, and social security, further impacting the working classes and the vulnerable.

AUSTERITY AND THE MOST VULNERABLE

In the post-crisis moments, capitalism's response often involves austerity policies that deepen social inequalities and increase difficulties for lower classes. Austerity, a set of measures aimed at reducing a country's budget deficit through cuts in public spending, is typically imposed in countries facing financial crises, often as a condition for receiving loans from international financial institutions.

However, austerity policies have disastrous consequences for the most vulnerable. When governments cut spending in essential areas like health, education, and infrastructure, it is the poorest populations that suffer the most. In Greece, for example, after the 2008 crisis, the IMF-imposed austerity led to the closure of hospitals, wage reductions, and the deterioration of living conditions for millions of citizens. Children lost access to quality public schools, the elderly were deprived of medical care, and young people faced high unemployment rates.

In other European and Latin American countries, austerity policies resulted in massive protests and social conflicts, as citizens began to realize that the financial crisis, caused by the greed of the wealthy and system failures, was being paid for by the poor population. These policies also resulted in a significant increase in social inequalities and wealth concentration in the hands of a small elite.

PERPETUAL POVERTY AND SOCIAL IMPACT

Economic crises, driven by capitalism's structural flaws, not only result in a temporary decline in living standards but have long-term effects. The poverty generated by these crises does not disappear quickly, and many countries struggle to fully recover. Social inequality becomes a vicious cycle, where generations most affected by the crises remain in a state of poverty or, at best, achieve only a marginal position in the labor market.

Moreover, economic crises have a devastating impact on the mental and physical health of populations. Unemployment, financial insecurity, and limited access to healthcare result in high levels of stress, depression, and poverty-related diseases such as malnutrition and chronic illnesses. Poorer communities, which already faced difficulties, become even more vulnerable and marginalized.

THE CAPITALIST SOLUTION: A CRISIS OF VALUATION?

Capitalism, in essence, lacks the capacity to prevent economic crises. They are inherent to the system itself, which relies on the constant pursuit of profit and the exploitation of resources and populations. The 1929 collapse, the 2008 crisis, and recurring economic insecurity demonstrate that the capitalist model, rather than being a solution to poverty, often perpetuates and amplifies it.

Austerity policies and financial bailouts for the wealthy are typical system responses, while the poor continue to bear the cost of market failures. Poverty, inequality, and marginalization are the products of a system that prioritizes profit and wealth concentration, rather than focusing on social well-being and providing opportunities for all.

CHAPTER 20: THE 1929 CRISIS – CAUSES, DEATHS, AND THE SHADOW OF WORLD WAR II

The 1929 Crisis, also known as the Great Depression, was one of the most devastating events in global economic history. Its consequences not only destroyed economies but also impacted lives, generated profound suffering, and, in many cases, resulted in deaths and global despair. What followed the collapse of the New York Stock Exchange was a chain of social and economic disasters that led to job losses, mass poverty, and a significant increase in inequality. Moreover, this crisis was not just an economic failure but also a crucial factor that set the stage for World War II, with political and social repercussions that shaped the course of the twentieth century.

THE CAUSE OF THE CRISIS: THE INSATIABLE PURSUIT OF PROFIT

The 1929 crisis was the culmination of a series of irresponsible economic practices and reckless speculation. In the years leading up to the crisis, the United States experienced a period of superficial prosperity. The 1920s became known as the *"Jazz Age"* or *"The Roaring Twenties"*, a time when the economy was rapidly growing and consumption seemed limitless. However, this growth was fueled by risky practices, including:

1. **Reckless Financial Speculation:**
   Investors bought stocks on the New York Stock Exchange without a realistic evaluation of company value. Instead of investing in businesses with solid foundations, many were merely betting on stock prices rising, creating a speculative bubble.

2. **Overproduction and Over-Indebtedness:**
   Industries were producing more than the market could consume, while families, encouraged by easy credit, bought more than they could pay for. This imbalance between production and consumption resulted in unsustainable stockpiles of unsold goods.

3. **Financial Deregulation:**
   The U.S. government adopted policies of deregulation, allowing the financial market to operate without proper oversight. Banks and investors allowed risky loans and speculative practices to proliferate without stability guarantees, setting the stage for an imminent collapse.

When trust in the market eroded and stock prices plummeted in 1929, panic took over. On October 29, 1929, known as *"Black Tuesday"*, the New York Stock Exchange collapsed. Investors sold stocks en masse, and the market's collapse led millions of Americans to bankruptcy.

THE CONSEQUENCES: POVERTY, DEATH, AND DESPAIR

The 1929 crisis not only destroyed companies but also deeply affected ordinary people's lives. Millions of citizens lost their savings, jobs, and, for many, their homes. The unemployment rate in the United States reached 25%, a historic mark that reflected the magnitude of the collapse. Individuals who lost jobs were forced to live on the streets, in makeshift camps called *"Hoovervilles"* (named after President Herbert Hoover), where conditions were extremely dire.

Food shortages became a serious problem, and many people died of starvation or malnutrition-related diseases. The lack of social assistance exacerbated the misery. Entire families were forced to abandon their homes, desperately seeking any means of survival.

The crisis also led to an increase in suicides, with thousands taking their lives due to the loss of everything they owned. Many businessmen, unable to cope with bankruptcy, resorted to suicide as a way to escape shame and hopelessness.

THE GLOBAL EFFECT: THE SPREAD OF THE CRISIS

The crisis was not limited to the United States. Countries around the world were equally devastated by the collapse of global trade and economic contraction. Germany, already trying to recover from the heavy burdens imposed by the Treaty of Versailles, saw its economy collapse. Unemployment and widespread poverty fueled popular discontent and the rise of extremist political movements, such as Nazism. Adolf Hitler, recognizing the population's dissatisfaction with the Weimar government, used the crisis as a platform to spread extreme nationalism and anti-Semitic rhetoric, securing public support for his rise to power.

In Latin America, the decline in global commodity markets and financial recession led to revolts and political instability. Brazil, for instance, faced a significant crisis in coffee exports, which resulted in protests and political changes.

THE HUMAN COST AND IMPACT ON GLOBAL POLITICS

The social impact of the 1929 crisis was devastating, with significant political and social repercussions. Discontent with living conditions and the loss of trust in liberal democracies contributed to the growth of authoritarian and totalitarian regimes worldwide. Populism and nationalism became tools for those seeking to restore stability, often resulting in fascist regimes and movements aiming to expand territories at the expense of other nations.

The 1929 crisis helped create conditions that would later lead to World War II. Economic instability and political radicalization were crucial components for the rise of dictators and militarists seeking to expand empires and resolve internal crises through war. Germany, under Adolf Hitler's leadership, found an opportunity to divert the population's attention from economic misery to a common enemy: Jews, Communists, and foreign powers.

Military expansion became a response to the crisis, and international conflicts began to take shape. European powers, such as Germany and Italy, attempted to rebuild their economies through territorial aggression, seeking resources and power to restore prosperity.

THE 1929 CRISIS AS EVIDENCE OF AN UNREGULATED CAPITALISM

The 1929 crisis exposed the structural flaws of unregulated capitalism. The relentless pursuit of profit, combined with the absence of a robust social safety net, generated a social and economic tragedy. The collapse of the New York Stock Exchange reflected the instability of the financial system, which prioritized the interests of a few over the well-being of many. The crisis spread quickly worldwide, resulting in suffering, death, and increased international tensions.

The 1929 crisis also highlighted that, in times of economic collapse, the poor and vulnerable are the most affected, while the wealthy can protect their fortunes or recover more quickly. Capitalism, in its relentless pursuit of profit, ignored the needs of the masses and set the stage for an even more turbulent future, with the emergence of totalitarian regimes and the rise of World War II.

This chapter seeks to detail how the 1929 crisis not only caused an economic catastrophe but also had a profound and lasting impact on global society, resulting in millions of deaths, fueling political radicalization, and ultimately becoming a central cause of World War II. Unregulated capitalism, in its quest for profit, sacrificed lives and destroyed economies, setting the stage for the political and social chaos that would follow.

CHAPTER 21: ENVIRONMENTALISM AND CAPITALISM – THE ENVIRONMENTAL DESTRUCTION CAUSED BY THE PURSUIT OF PROFIT

Capitalism, throughout its history, has been a powerful engine of economic progress but also a destructive force for the environment. The relentless pursuit of profit and growth has led to the unsustainable exploitation of the planet's natural resources. The drive to maximize profits, often without considering environmental costs, has generated devastating impacts on Earth. From the Industrial Revolution to the modern world, capitalism has been inseparable from environmental destruction, creating a cycle of excessive consumption and ecosystem degradation.

Capitalism and the Exploitation of Natural Resources

At the heart of capitalism lies the need for continuous expansion – more production, more consumption, and consequently, more exploitation of natural resources. The Industrial Revolution, with its focus on large-scale production and new technologies, was a historical milestone that transformed the planet but also accelerated the process of environmental destruction. Forests were cut down, mines were opened, rivers and lakes were polluted – all in the name of progress and profit generation.

Natural resources, once seen as abundant and infinite, have become mere commodities to be exploited until exhaustion. Oil, coal, natural gas, and other minerals have become the pillars of a growing industrial economy. Large-scale agriculture and intensive livestock farming also took over vast areas of land, destroying natural habitats and disrupting ecological cycles.

The Environmental Impact of Exploitation

The capitalist system, with its intensive production model, not only depletes natural resources but also leaves a legacy of pollution and climate change. What began with the burning of coal to fuel the machines of the Industrial Revolution has turned into a massive pollutant-emitting machine, with the burning of fossil fuels becoming the main cause of global warming. The uncontrolled use of pesticides and fertilizers in industrial agriculture also contributes to soil contamination and biodiversity loss.

Moreover, practices such as mining and deforestation have caused irreversible environmental damage. Large areas of tropical forests, like the Amazon, have been decimated to make way for monocultures and cattle ranching. The loss of these forests not only affects biodiversity but also exacerbates global warming since forests act as carbon reservoirs, absorbing large amounts of carbon dioxide from the atmosphere.

Environmental Inequality

Although environmental damage is a global issue, the impacts are not distributed equally. Poor countries and communities often suffer the most from the environmental consequences of capitalism. Developing nations are frequently used as dumping grounds for toxic waste, industrial landfills, and areas for natural resource extraction, with little or no environmental protection. An example of this is the way many countries in Africa, Latin America, and Asia suffer from the extraction of minerals like gold, diamonds, and oil, where the benefits of this exploitation are concentrated in the hands of large multinational corporations, while local populations face water contamination, air pollution, and land destruction.

Furthermore, climate change, exacerbated by the unchecked emission of greenhouse gases, disproportionately affects vulnerable communities. Indigenous peoples, who live in harmony with the environment, are often the first victims of deforestation and the degradation of their territories, losing their homes, culture, and way of life.

The Cost of Nature: Negative Externalities

In capitalism, environmental costs are often not accounted for in company balance sheets. These negative externalities – such as pollution, deforestation, and biodiversity loss – are ignored or minimized, while the profits from exploiting natural resources are maximized. The concept of "economic growth" in capitalism often overlooks the fact that land and its resources are finite.

Large companies, in their pursuit of profit, frequently prefer to cut costs by avoiding investment in clean technologies or sustainable practices. They externalize environmental costs onto the public, which ultimately bears the burden, either through air and water pollution or through the loss of quality of life and increased diseases related to these factors.

The Search for Solutions: Environmentalism vs. Capitalism

Although environmental degradation is largely a consequence of capitalism, there is a growing movement that proposes solutions aimed at mitigating the damages caused. Environmentalism is gaining strength, with more voices demanding a change in the economic development model. However, the proposed solutions often conflict with the fundamental principles of capitalism, which seek to maximize profit and economic growth.

Green capitalism, an attempt to reconcile profit with environmental preservation, has been widely criticized. While some practices, such as adopting renewable energy sources and corporate social responsibility, may contribute to a more sustainable economy, many critics argue that these initiatives are insufficient to reverse the damages caused by the capitalist model of excessive exploitation.

The Need for a New Model

The environmental destruction caused by the insatiable pursuit of profit is a reflection of the failures of capitalism, which prioritizes economic growth over the preservation of life on the planet. The development model based on the reckless exploitation of natural resources is exhausted, and climate change is proof of this. For a real change to happen, it is necessary to rethink how we deal with the economy and nature. The future of the planet depends on our ability to break with this model and adopt an approach that places sustainability and equity first.

The transition to a sustainable and just economy will require profound changes, not only in environmental policies but also in how companies operate, how governments regulate, and how people perceive consumption and economic growth. Only then can we ensure that the damages caused by capitalism can be reversed and that the planet can sustain future generations.

This chapter explored how capitalism, with its relentless pursuit of profit, has been the driving force of environmental destruction, exacerbating issues such as climate change, biodiversity loss, and the exploitation of natural resources. The environmental impact of capitalism is one of the most urgent issues of our time, requiring a deep reflection on the development model we have followed and the necessary alternatives to protect the Earth.

CHAPTER 22: THE ROLE OF MAJOR CORPORATIONS IN GLOBAL WARMING

Major corporations play a central role in global warming and the environmental crises that plague the planet. Their relentless pursuit of profit at any cost, without proper social and environmental responsibility, has contributed significantly to the acceleration of climate change. These companies, particularly the giants in the fossil fuel, mining, agriculture, and chemical industries, are responsible for a substantial portion of greenhouse gas emissions that drive global warming. However, throughout history, they have managed to avoid full accountability by manipulating legislation, denying scientific evidence, and engaging in **greenwashing**—practices aimed at creating a false image of sustainability.

THE IMPACT OF FOSSIL FUEL INDUSTRIES

The oil, gas, and coal industries are the primary contributors to carbon dioxide (CO_2) and methane (CH_4) emissions, two of the most harmful greenhouse gases to the climate. These corporations, which generate billions in profits, have a history of minimizing environmental damage and sabotaging public policies aimed at controlling emissions. Companies like **ExxonMobil, Shell, and BP** have been widely criticized for their role in global warming, not only due to the extraction and burning of fossil fuels but also through their involvement in misinformation campaigns to discredit climate science. Oil extraction and coal mining, aside from causing pollution, often result in ecological disasters such as leaks and spills that affect oceans, rivers, and entire ecosystems.

AGRICULTURE AND DEFORESTATION

The agricultural industry, particularly soybean farming, biofuel production, and intensive livestock farming, also plays a significant role in global warming. These large-scale activities generate methane emissions (a greenhouse gas far more potent than CO_2) and cause massive deforestation, especially in regions like the **Amazon, Indonesia, and other tropical areas**. Expanding agricultural borders to make room for commodities like soy and meat destroys tropical forests and other vital ecosystems that act as **carbon sinks**, absorbing CO_2 from the atmosphere. Instead of protecting these areas crucial to climate stability, major corporations view these lands solely as sources of profit.

CHEMICAL CORPORATIONS AND TOXIC POLLUTION

Chemical companies, with their massive use of pesticides, synthetic fertilizers, and other toxic substances, also have significant environmental impacts. Besides contaminating soil and water, these companies often engage in irresponsible production practices, neglecting long-term environmental and human health impacts. The widespread use of **agrochemicals in monoculture farming** compromises biodiversity and directly affects local communities' health, particularly in vulnerable areas across **Africa, Asia, and Latin America**.

THE POLITICS OF MAJOR CORPORATIONS: GREENWASHING AND POLITICAL INFLUENCE

Despite their environmentally harmful practices, many corporations attempt to project an image of environmental responsibility, a practice known as **greenwashing**. They promote initiatives like emission reduction, renewable energy use, and tree planting, but these actions are often insufficient to offset the environmental damage caused by their core operations. Some companies claim carbon neutrality goals but continue predatory activities. Additionally, these corporations often wield significant political influence, funding lobbies and supporting governments that downplay or ignore environmental issues, thereby delaying or blocking crucial legislation to combat global warming.

ECOLOGICAL DISASTERS AND IRREPARABLE DAMAGE

The activities of major corporations not only contribute to global warming but also cause devastating ecological disasters that result in irreparable environmental damage. These disasters, often ignored or minimized by responsible companies, have catastrophic effects on human populations and ecosystems.

The Bhopal Disaster (India) – 1984

The Bhopal disaster, one of the worst industrial accidents in history, occurred when a **Union Carbide plant leaked toxic gas (methyl isocyanate)**, killing thousands of people and leaving hundreds of thousands of survivors with serious health issues. This disaster highlights corporations' lack of responsibility regarding safety and environmental impact, especially in developing countries where **environmental regulations are weaker**.

Oil Spills and Chemical Leaks

Oil spills, such as the **Exxon Valdez incident in 1989** and the **recent BP spill in the Gulf of Mexico**, cause devastating damage to marine ecosystems, wildlife, and local economies that rely on the ocean for **fishing and tourism**. Furthermore, chemical leaks and toxic pollution continue to affect rivers and soil worldwide, rendering some areas uninhabitable and irreversibly damaged.

THE COLLAPSE OF NATURAL ECOSYSTEMS

Predatory extraction practices are decimating entire ecosystems. Mining operations for **gold and diamonds** have destroyed forests and farmland, while ongoing deforestation continues to advance in tropical regions, affecting local flora and fauna. Climate change caused by the burning of fossil fuels has led to extreme climate shifts, such as **droughts, floods, and storms**, resulting in the deaths of millions and the displacement of thousands more.

CONCLUSION: THE FUTURE OF CAPITALISM

Capitalism, in its relentless pursuit of profit, has been one of the main drivers of **environmental destruction and ecological crises**. The unchecked exploitation of natural resources, pollution, and global warming lie at the heart of the environmental problems we face today. While there are some attempts to transition to **green capitalism**, these solutions are often insufficient in the face of the scale of damage caused.

The future of capitalism, especially in its current form, is **unsustainable**. To ensure the survival of the planet and future generations, it is necessary to **reimagine the global economic system**, with a focus on **sustainability, social equity, and collective well-being**, rather than profit at any cost. Otherwise, capitalism, as we know it, may become one of the leading causes of **environmental destruction and species extinction**, including our own. The challenge lies in reversing the damage and creating an economic model that respects the planet's **limits and prioritizes humanity's needs** over the profits of a few corporations.

CHAPTER 23: REFLECTION ON ALTERNATIVES TO THE CURRENT SYSTEM

Capitalism, as the dominant economic system, has generated devastating consequences for the environment, societies, and individuals, particularly those who are most vulnerable. In light of these damages, reflections on the need for alternatives to this system are growing. Social and economic movements around the world have risen against the abuses and inequalities created by capitalism, seeking solutions for a fairer, more sustainable, and equitable future. This chapter explores some of these alternatives, as well as the role of social and economic movements in building a more just world.

THE CURRENT SYSTEM AND ITS LIMITS

Capitalism, in its neoliberal form, is based on the idea that a free market, without state intervention, can create a prosperous society where everyone benefits. However, evidence shows that this system not only fails to combat inequality but also perpetuates exploitation, wealth concentration, and the impoverishment of populations. Economic crises, environmental degradation, increasing violence, and disregard for human rights are just a few of the failures that make the continuation of the capitalist model increasingly unsustainable.

Capitalism is also tied to the relentless pursuit of profit, without considering the planet's limits and human needs. The logic of exploiting natural resources, rampant consumption, and structural inequality ends up creating a system of winners and losers, where most people are marginalized and impoverished while a minority concentrates power, wealth, and influence.

ALTERNATIVES TO CAPITALISM: WHAT IS BEING PROPOSED?

1. Solidarity Economy

One of the most significant alternatives to capitalism is the idea of a solidarity economy, which aims to create economic systems based on cooperation, solidarity, and social well-being. Instead of prioritizing profit, the solidarity economy seeks to promote equality, respect for the environment, and social justice. Worker cooperatives, social enterprises, and local markets are examples of practices that aim to create a more humane economy, where people's needs are met rather than the interests of large corporations.

2. Ecosocialism

Ecosocialism is a movement that integrates social and environmental solutions to the problems caused by capitalism. It advocates for an economy based on public control of natural resources, wealth redistribution, and the promotion of social and environmental justice. Ecosocialism proposes a paradigm shift, where production and consumption are focused on collective well-being and sustainability, in contrast to individual profit and environmental destruction.

Ecosocialism also critiques the idea of endless economic growth, a pillar of capitalism, and proposes a more balanced vision, where societies can prosper sustainably while respecting the planet's ecological limits. The focus is on building a more egalitarian society, where everyone has access to the resources needed to live with dignity.

3. Green Economy

Although capitalism is at the root of environmental destruction, the green economy offers an alternative that attempts to reconcile economic development with environmental respect.

This alternative focuses on sustainable technologies, renewable energies, and more responsible consumption models. The idea is to reduce the ecological footprint of human activities and promote the transition to clean energy sources, such as solar and wind power, while encouraging recycling and material reuse.

However, critics of the green economy argue that, on its own, this alternative may be insufficient, as it often does not question capitalism's foundations, such as consumerism and inequality. It may end up merely "greening" capitalist practices without truly transforming the underlying economic model.

4. Democratic Socialism and Communism

Democratic socialism and communism offer more radical alternatives, with an approach aimed at eliminating the structural inequalities caused by capitalism. Democratic socialism proposes an economy based on collective or publicly controlled ownership, where production is organized democratically and resources are redistributed to reduce wealth disparities. The central idea is that the means of production (factories, land, companies) should be collectively owned rather than controlled by a corporate minority, as is the case in capitalism.

Communism, in its classical vision, seeks a classless society, where the production and distribution of goods are organized collectively, and everyone has equal access to resources. Although communism has been implemented in authoritarian forms in some countries, many strands of democratic socialism believe that the model can be achieved through democratic political processes, with popular participation and a diversity of opinions.

SOCIAL AND ECONOMIC MOVEMENTS AGAINST CAPITALIST ABUSES

1. Labor Movements

Labor movements have been crucial in fighting against capitalist abuses. Workers, historically exploited and marginalized, have organized into unions and movements to secure better working conditions, fair wages, and social rights. Additionally, protests against labor reforms and the privatization of essential services are part of the struggle against the abuses of the capitalist system.

2. Indigenous and Environmental Movements

Indigenous and environmental movements have been at the forefront of resistance against the destructive impacts of capitalism, particularly in relation to natural resource exploitation and environmental degradation. These movements expose the abuses of corporations and the state, which often plunder indigenous lands in the name of profit. The fight for land rights, forest preservation, and combating deforestation is central to these movements, which seek to reverse the impact caused by large companies' expansion into the global market.

3. Global Justice Movements

Organizations like the Global Social Justice Movement expose the negative impacts of globalization and neoliberal policies, which favor economic powers at the expense of poorer countries. These movements fight against fossil fuel imperialism, austerity policies, external debt, and global inequalities. They advocate for a fairer and more equal economic model, where people's needs are prioritized over corporate interests.

CONCLUSION

The alternatives to capitalism are not merely theoretical but are being lived and practiced by various social movements around the world. However, these alternatives still face significant resistance from the forces that dominate capitalism. For the changes proposed by these alternatives to be effectively implemented, a global collective effort will be necessary to challenge existing power structures and promote a deep transformation in economic, social, and political systems.

Capitalism, in its current state, is reaching a critical point, and the proposed alternatives offer the chance to reverse the damages caused and build a fairer, more sustainable, and equitable world. The struggle continues and depends on the mobilization of all those who believe in a better future for generations to come.

CHAPTER 24: HOW ECONOMIC INEQUALITY CREATES MOST OF THE VIOLENCE

Economic inequality is one of the most significant factors in the creation of social violence. In capitalist societies, where the gap between the rich and the poor is accentuated, violence becomes an almost inevitable byproduct. Although violence has multiple causes, extreme poverty, lack of access to opportunities, and the absence of an effective social protection system are often the main reasons for the emergence of crimes such as drug trafficking, robberies, kidnappings, and even hate crimes.

Economic Inequality and the Rise of Organized Crime

In a capitalist system, the inequalities in access to resources and opportunities generate profound frustration and alienation, especially among the lower classes of society. When someone is born into extreme poverty with few prospects for improvement, the path of crime becomes one of the perceived alternatives to achieving a better life. This scenario is further exacerbated in areas where the state fails to provide security, quality education, and healthcare.

Drug trafficking is a clear example of how economic inequality contributes to the growth of crime. The drug market offers high profits for traffickers, and due to a lack of opportunities, many young people from impoverished neighborhoods see involvement in this illegal trade as the only way to improve their lives. Gangs and criminal factions, often operating with heavy weaponry, become a direct reflection of the absence of infrastructure and viable alternatives.

Moreover, the living conditions in slums and impoverished areas create an environment conducive to the spread of crime. The presence of criminal factions controlling drug distribution, extortions, robberies, and even arms trafficking becomes a logical consequence of a socially unequal structure. Violence, then, becomes a method of maintaining control over territories and resources, exacerbated by economic marginalization.

Corruption and Institutional Violence

Violence also manifests in the actions of the state itself, which often responds in a brutal and disproportionate manner to social protests. Police repression and the excessive use of force in impoverished areas, where residents face poor living conditions, create a cycle of institutional violence. Economic inequality, therefore, fuels violence at both the individual and institutional levels.

This relationship between inequality and violence is not an isolated phenomenon but is widely present in any society with a significant wealth disparity. When people feel excluded and deprived of basic resources, they resort to violence, often as a form of protest against the system that oppresses them.

Conclusion

In summary, economic inequality is not only a flaw of the capitalist system but also one of the primary causes of violence that pervades various societies around the world. Capitalism, by concentrating wealth and leaving vast populations in extreme poverty, creates an environment ripe for the emergence of crimes and the perpetuation of an endless cycle of violence.

CHAPTER 25: WHY CAPITALISM NEEDS ECONOMIC INEQUALITY TO EXIST

One of the central characteristics of capitalism is economic inequality. It is not an unwanted byproduct but an intrinsic necessity for the system's functioning. At its core, capitalism relies on the concentration of wealth in the hands of a few to ensure the operation of the market, the perpetuation of the economic model, and the maintenance of social order.

Capitalism and Wealth Accumulation

At the heart of capitalism lies the idea of capital accumulation. In a capitalist system, profit is generated through the exploitation of labor, large-scale production, and the maximization of efficiency. For the system to function efficiently, it is necessary for a large segment of the population to be in a vulnerable position, which allows capital to be accumulated by a small elite.

Economic inequality is essential to the operation of the law of supply and demand. If everyone had the same opportunities, competition in the labor market and in the production of goods and services would become more balanced, and profit margins would be significantly lower. The concentration of wealth in a few hands creates a class of consumers with high purchasing power and, simultaneously, a mass of workers who depend on the decisions of large business owners for their survival.

Exploitation of Labor and Perpetuation of Inequality

Economic inequality is fueled by the exploitation of labor. Capitalism is built on the idea that part of the population must work for another part, with owners of the means of production keeping the majority of the profit. To achieve this, it is necessary for the working class to have limited access to education, healthcare, and other resources, which restricts their social mobility and prevents them from competing on an equal footing.

However, inequality is not just a feature of capitalism but a requirement for its existence. It ensures that workers continue to produce goods and services while capital owners continue to accumulate wealth. This cycle of exploitation is the backbone of a system that, ultimately, is sustained by inequality.

Capitalism and Social Order

In addition to being an economic imperative, inequality also plays a crucial role in maintaining social order. Capitalism, by promoting competition and class division, creates a system in which elites can maintain control over the masses. By establishing a hierarchical system where access to power, wealth, and resources is limited, capitalism ensures that the dominant class continues to govern without significant resistance.

Inequality also prevents workers from uniting to challenge the system, as the differing interests between classes create a barrier to communication and solidarity. Moreover, the constant economic pressure keeps the population focused on the struggle for survival, diverting attention away from a deeper critique of the capitalist system itself.

Conclusion

Therefore, capitalism is not just an economic system that tolerates inequality; it depends on it to function. Inequality is a structural and necessary characteristic for wealth accumulation, labor exploitation, and social order maintenance. Without inequality, capitalism would not be able to operate efficiently, and the economic powers that sustain this system would lose their dominance.

CHAPTER 26: THE FUTILITY VICES CAUSED BY CAPITALISM: THE NEED FOR ETERNAL COMPETITION

Capitalism promotes a society based on superficial values, where a person's worth is often measured by what they own, the status they display, and their position on the social ladder. This system of constant competition and comparison fuels a cycle of dissatisfaction and existential emptiness, as people are driven to believe that they need more to become more, in an endless pursuit of social approval and external validation.

The Eternal Competition and the Pursuit of Success

By placing competition at the center of social life, capitalism creates a scenario where every individual feels the need to constantly outdo themselves, not only in terms of skills and competence but also in terms of the material possessions they own. The idea that having more means being more permeates all layers of society, from workers to elites, leading to a continuous comparison with others.

This competition manifests in the relentless quest for social status, which is reflected in comparisons of jobs, houses, cars, and fashion. The capitalist society promotes the notion that happiness and success are measured by the accumulation of material goods. The idea of needing the best car, the most expensive house, and the most prestigious job is deeply rooted in the capitalist mindset.

Alienation and Existential Emptiness

Capitalism also fosters a sense of alienation among people, who, in their pursuit of reaching the top, become disconnected from their true needs and desires. The quest for external perfection creates an existential void, where individuals, in their desire for more, end up feeling dissatisfied and disconnected from their own lives and emotions. Human relationships become based on the exchange of material goods and competition rather than affection or solidarity.

The Need for Consumption and Superficial Values

Capitalism also generates a consumer-driven society, where happiness is constantly tied to the consumption of new products and the acquisition of things. Advertising and marketing fuel the belief that purchasing products from well-known or luxury brands is a way to achieve an ideal life, creating a mindset of scarcity and a constant need for consumption. This results in a disconnection between true human needs and the needs created by the system, perpetuating a culture of continuous dissatisfaction.

CHAPTER 26: THE RISE OF THE USA AS A WORLD POWER AND THE IMPACTS OF ECONOMIC CONTROL

The United States rose to become the world's leading power in the 20th century, consolidating economic and political dominance that transformed the country into the main influencer of international relations and the controller of the global financial system. This position was achieved through strategies that included advantageous economic agreements, the establishment of the dollar as the global reference currency, and the use of sanctions and economic blockades against nations that opposed American interests.

HOW THE USA BECAME THE LEADING WORLD POWER

1. World War II and the Marshall Plan

After World War II, while Europe lay in ruins, the USA emerged as one of the few industrialized countries that remained intact and prosperous. The Marshall Plan, which financed the reconstruction of Western Europe, ensured that the benefiting countries became economically and politically dependent on the USA. This also established the dollar as the preferred currency for international transactions.

2. The Bretton Woods Agreement (1944)

The Bretton Woods system fixed the dollar as the main international reserve currency, tied to gold. This privileged position gave the USA a unique economic advantage: they could print the currency that the world needed for global trade. Although the gold standard was abandoned in 1971, the dollar continued to be the dominant currency.

3. The Military-Industrial Complex

The USA invested vast resources into developing its military apparatus and defense industry, which not only solidified its leadership role militarily but also boosted its economy. With military bases around the world and direct influence over organizations like NATO, the USA reinforced its role as the "guardians" of global order.

USING SANCTIONS AND BLOCKADES TO CONTROL OTHER COUNTRIES

The USA has a long history of using economic sanctions and trade blockades as weapons against nations that challenge its dominance. These measures often result in economic collapse, exacerbating social and political crises. Although these sanctions are presented as actions to "promote democracy" or "punish authoritarian regimes," they often serve to protect American economic and political interests.

Cuba: Economic Blockade and Isolation

Since 1962, the USA has imposed an economic blockade against Cuba, prohibiting trade and financial transactions with the country. This caused severe shortages of essential goods, technology, and investments, restricting Cuba's economic growth. While the USA claims the blockade aims to pressure the Cuban government into adopting democratic reforms, it has, in practice, caused suffering for the population while preventing the spread of an alternative socialist economic model in the region.

Venezuela: Sanctions and Economic Crisis

American sanctions against Venezuela, especially after 2014, significantly worsened the country's economic crisis. These measures blocked oil exports, the main source of Venezuelan revenue, and isolated the nation from the global financial system. Although internal mismanagement also contributed to economic problems, American sanctions undeniably deepened the poverty and suffering.

Russia: Economic Restrictions and International Isolation

Sanctions against Russia, intensified after the annexation of Crimea in 2014 and more recently due to the Ukraine conflict, aimed to restrict Russia's access to advanced technologies, financial markets, and global trade. While these sanctions weakened strategic sectors of the Russian economy, they also impacted European economies dependent on Russian natural gas, demonstrating how the USA manipulates the global system for its benefit.

MANIPULATING THE DOLLAR AND THE IMPACT ON GLOBAL ECONOMIES

The dollar, as the global reserve currency, serves as a tool of American economic control. Because it dominates trade transactions and central bank reserves, the USA holds disproportionate power over the international financial system. The USA manipulates this position to impose its political and economic will, negatively affecting countries that do not follow its guidelines.

- **Devaluation and Monetary Sanctions:** The USA can freeze dollar assets from countries considered adversaries, such as Russia, Iran, and Venezuela, effectively paralyzing their economies.

- **Manipulating Interest Rates:** Changes in American monetary policies directly impact other economies, particularly those reliant on external financing in dollars.

- **Control of the SWIFT System:** By controlling the SWIFT international payment system, the USA can exclude countries from global trade, as they did with Iran.

WHO IS TRULY RESPONSIBLE FOR POVERTY AND MISERY?

The USA often blames local governments for poverty in countries like Venezuela, Cuba, and Russia, but their sanctions and restrictive policies play a central role in worsening these crises. By isolating these nations from global trade and limiting their revenue sources, the USA ensures they remain in poverty while promoting their own dominance as the solution to "underdevelopment."

- **Cuba:** The poverty and difficulties faced by the Cuban people are largely attributed to the economic blockade, which stifles the country's development.

- **Venezuela:** Although internal mismanagement contributed to the crisis, American sanctions severely restricted the nation's economic options.

- **Russia:** The sanctions imposed after 2014 aim to weaken the Russian economy and its global influence, also harming its population.

CONCLUSION

The USA consolidated its global power through economic and political strategies that not only secure its dominance but also perpetuate poverty and underdevelopment in countries that resist its influence. The use of the dollar as an economic weapon and the imposition of sanctions and blockades make the USA a central contributor to the suffering of many nations. This unchecked control over the global economic system calls into question the legitimacy of a model that enriches a few at the expense of many.

CHAPTER 27: CELEBRITIES FOR SALE: THE ENTERTAINMENT INDUSTRY AND THE CAPITALISM OF APPEARANCE

At the heart of capitalism, celebrities emerge as one of the most powerful tools to sustain the system. They not only reflect the values of a consumer-driven society but are also strategically used to shape behaviors, influence desires, and perpetuate the relentless profit dynamics. More than artists or influencers, celebrities are carefully manufactured products designed to serve economic interests.

THE PRODUCT: THE MANUFACTURED IMAGE

From the beginning of their careers, celebrities are shaped by marketing teams, stylists, and agents who create personalities strategically designed to attract specific audiences. This process transforms individuals into brands that sell dreams and lifestyles. This fabrication is not just a market strategy but a tool of capitalism to create aspirants — people who yearn to consume products or styles that bring them closer to their idols.

Capitalism uses celebrities to reinforce the idea that happiness, success, and beauty are achievable through consumption. They become living showcases of products, fashion, and experiences, making fans desire something often out of reach.

THE SURVEILLANCE CAPITALISM: LIFE AS A REALITY SHOW

The constant surveillance of celebrities' lives — by paparazzi, tabloids, and social media — is not just entertainment but a model of capitalist exploitation. Every aspect of their lives is monetized: weddings, divorces, births, mental health crises. Even their vulnerabilities are transformed into commodities that generate clicks, views, and sales.

This dynamic not only dehumanizes artists but also creates a toxic cycle for consumers. The obsession with celebrity life fuels the need to acquire products that promise a connection to this glamorous world, even if only on a superficial level.

TOOLS OF SOCIAL MANIPULATION

The use of celebrities as tools of capitalism extends beyond selling products. They are employed to legitimize economic and social systems that perpetuate inequalities. By promoting an image of success and personal fulfillment, celebrities reinforce the false narrative that capitalism offers equal opportunities to everyone.

This illusion masks structural inequalities and diverts attention from systemic injustices. While millions struggle to survive, celebrities serve as a distraction, perpetuating a cycle where a few thrive at the expense of widespread exploitation.

EXPLOITATION AND CONTROL IN THE ENTERTAINMENT CAPITALISM

The idea that celebrities are free and powerful is often an illusion. Record labels, studios, and agencies control fundamental aspects of their lives, from contracts that dictate how they should dress to who they can publicly associate with. Their personalities are often manufactured, friendships are strategically managed, and their behaviors are closely monitored.

Examples like Britney Spears, who lived under a controlling conservatorship for years, reveal how capitalism treats celebrities as investments. It's not about who they are but what they can generate in profit.

THE MALADY OF CAPITALISM: CREATING INSATIABLE CONSUMERS

Capitalism uses celebrities to create and reinforce the idea that happiness comes through consumption. This turns society into a cycle of chronic dissatisfaction: no one is beautiful, rich, or famous enough, but one can always strive to be, through more consumption.

Celebrities, as tools of the system, feed this dynamic. They promote disposable fashion products, unattainable beauty standards, and luxurious lifestyles — all of which only reinforce the dissatisfaction of their followers.

CONCLUSION: CELEBRITIES AS INSTRUMENTS OF THE SYSTEM

Celebrities are not only victims of capitalism but also essential components of its machinery. Transformed into icons of an idealized life, they help to mask the real flaws of the system, distracting society from the inequalities and injustices it perpetuates. Capitalism appropriates their images, their lives, and even their suffering to fuel an endless cycle of consumption.

Thus, the glitz of Hollywood and the glamour of stars hide a darker truth: in the end, everything is shaped by profit, and celebrities are just another commodity on the capitalist shelf.

CHAPTER 28: PROPAGANDA AS A WEAPON OF AMERICAN CAPITALISM

Since the early 20th century, the United States has used culture and media as strategic tools to shape the global perception of countries that challenge its economic and geopolitical interests. This practice, based on the manipulation of narratives, legitimizes wars, sanctions, and interventionist policies, while concealing the true objectives behind these actions.

STEREOTYPES IN POPULAR CULTURE

Hollywood films and TV shows frequently portray Middle Eastern people as terrorists, Chinese individuals as spies or dictators, and Cubans as oppressors. These narratives create deeply entrenched biases that justify military and economic interventions, as well as reinforce the idea that the U.S. is the "hero" fighting for freedom and democracy.

THE DEMONIZATION OF POLITICAL ENEMIES

- **Middle East:** After the September 11 attacks, the "war on terror" was used to legitimize invasions in Afghanistan and Iraq. Media narratives reinforced the idea that the entire Middle East was a threat, while hiding the oil interests behind these actions.

- **Cuba:** Portrayed as an oppressive and failed regime, Cuba endures sanctions that are the real cause of its poverty, while the U.S. promotes the narrative that socialism is to blame.

- **China:** Often accused of authoritarian practices, China is depicted as a global threat to justify trade barriers, sanctions, and the militarization of Asia.

THE JUSTIFICATION FOR WARS AND SANCTIONS

By creating villains in global narratives, the U.S. gains internal and international support for interventions. The fear of "threats to democracy" or "terrorism" is used to conceal objectives such as controlling natural resources, markets, and areas of influence.

GLOBAL IMPACT

This strategy not only stigmatizes nations and cultures but also causes economic and social suffering in target countries. Economic blockades, such as those imposed on Cuba and Venezuela, perpetuate crises, while wars and interventions leave behind destruction under the pretext of "protecting freedom."

CONCLUSION

American propaganda is a powerful weapon of capitalism, manipulating narratives to secure global control and economic dominance. This practice does not reflect a pursuit of democracy or peace, but rather the maintenance of a system that benefits corporate elites at the expense of millions of lives. As Malcolm X said: *"If you're not careful, newspapers will have you hating the people who are oppressed and loving the people who oppress them."*

CHAPTER 29: THE MARKET AND ITS REACTION — A MIRROR OF THE POWERFUL

The financial market is often presented as the thermometer of a country's economic health. When stock markets rise and the dollar falls, analysts celebrate. When the opposite occurs, alarms sound. But the truth is that these metrics reveal very little about the real well-being of the population. In practice, the market is a reflection of the interests of financial elites, not general prosperity.

THE BEHAVIOR OF THE MARKET: FAVORITISM AND PUNISHMENT

The market acts almost immediately to influence political decisions, and its response is often biased:

- **When governments favor workers** by increasing wages, strengthening unions, or expanding social programs, the market reacts negatively. The dollar rises, the country's risk increases, and investors warn of "economic instability." These reactions send a clear message that the financial system prioritizes cost control (especially workforce costs) over social well-being.

- **When policies favor entrepreneurs and banks**, such as tax cuts for large corporations or the relaxation of labor laws, the market responds with euphoria. The appreciation of the local currency and the stability of indices are presented as proof that the economy is doing well, even if social indicators show the opposite.

THE FALLACY OF ECONOMIC INDICATORS

Indices like GDP, inflation, and the stock market are widely used to measure a country's economic success. However, these numbers rarely say much about the quality of life for the majority of the population.

- **GDP growth can coexist with increasing inequality.** A country may become wealthier overall, but if wealth distribution is unequal, most people will continue to live in poor conditions.

- **Low inflation can hide stagnant wages.** Keeping prices low at the cost of workers' purchasing power is not progress; it is social control.

- **Rising stock markets reflect corporate profits, not popular prosperity.** Large companies can profit even during crises by exploiting cheap labor and natural resources.

THE DICTATORSHIP OF THE MARKET

The market has become a coercive tool used to steer public policies. Governments that challenge financial interests are punished with "capital flight" and currency devaluation, creating a cycle of dependency and submission to the wealthy elite.

A clear example is the role of credit rating agencies, which often downgrade the credit rating of countries that invest in social policies, while upgrading the ratings of countries that adopt austerity measures, even if these actions result in population suffering.

WHO TRULY BENEFITS?

When the market claims that a country is "doing well," it's crucial to ask: for whom? Brazil, for instance, serves as a prime example:

- **During periods when the dollar fell and the market celebrated**, such as the privatization era in the 1990s, inequality increased, and essential sectors like health and education were dismantled.

- **When public policies supported the poor**, such as strengthening the minimum wage and social programs, the market reacted with pessimism, even though the population experienced significant improvements in their quality of life.

CONCLUSION: THE MARKET DOES NOT REPRESENT THE POPULATION

At its core, the market is a tool of capitalism. It measures success according to the interests of large investors, corporations, and banks, while ignoring the impact of policies on the majority of the population.

It is necessary to demystify the idea that a "rising market" signifies real progress. As economist Thomas Piketty said:

"The market by itself never balances inequalities; on the contrary, it deepens them."

The true indicator of a nation's success should be the quality of life of its people, not the satisfaction of a financial elite that profits at the expense of exploiting the majority.

CHAPTER 30: THE FUTURE WE CHOOSE

Capitalism, with all its promises of progress and prosperity, has proven to be a double-edged sword. While it has enabled scientific, technological, and economic advancements, it has also brought about inequality, environmental destruction, human exploitation, and recurring crises that shake the foundations of civilization.

This book has sought to expose the hidden side of a system that dominates the world but does not always work in the interest of its inhabitants. The question that remains is not only about how we got here but about what future we want to build from this point forward.

REFLECTION ON THE SYSTEM

Capitalism, like all human systems, is not immutable. It was created, shaped, and refined through historical decisions, economic interests, and political conveniences. Therefore, it can also be transformed. But this requires the courage to question the status quo, the boldness to propose alternatives, and, above all, the solidarity to envision a world where profit is not the only driving force behind our actions.

"The history of any society up to the present day is the history of class struggle," said Karl Marx, warning of the divisions that economic systems create. In capitalism, the struggle is not only between social classes but also between the planet itself and those who exploit it.

INDIVIDUAL AND COLLECTIVE RESPONSIBILITY

Each of us, as consumers and citizens, has a role in this system. Although our individual choices may seem small, they reflect values that, collectively, can shape society. Conscious consumption, political engagement, and the pursuit of economic alternatives are necessary steps to challenge the established order.

However, it is not enough to act individually. We must fight for policies that promote equity, corporations that respect the environment and human rights, and leaders who prioritize the well-being of people over profits.

THE CHOICE THAT DEFINES TOMORROW

Capitalism, as we know it, is not sustainable in the long run. Whether through environmental destruction, the perpetuation of inequality, or increasing economic instability, it is heading toward a breaking point. The question is not whether the system will change, but how and under what conditions this change will occur.

We can choose to continue down a path of exploitation and inequality, or we can work together to create a system that prioritizes justice, sustainability, and the common good.

A QUOTE TO REFLECT ON

We end with a quote from Albert Einstein, who, despite being known for his contributions to science, was also a keen critic of the capitalist system:

"We cannot solve our problems with the same thinking we used when we created them."

Change begins with the courage to think differently and the determination to act collectively. The future of capitalism — and the world — is in our hands.

Bonus Chapter: The Golden Calf and Religious Contradiction

From the earliest times, humanity has grappled with the dilemma between the pursuit of wealth and spiritual values. The Bible contains numerous passages condemning attachment to money and material possessions, often warning about the dangers of this obsession. However, throughout history, the very institution that championed these teachings amassed incalculable fortunes, consolidating one of the greatest paradoxes of Christian faith.

THE GOLDEN CALF: A SYMBOL OF HUMAN GREED

In the Book of Exodus, the story of the Golden Calf stands out as one of the most emblematic accounts of idolatry and wealth. After Moses ascended Mount Sinai to receive the Ten Commandments, the impatient Israelites persuaded Aaron to create a golden idol for them to worship. They melted their jewelry and valuable items, crafting a golden statue that symbolized not just a religious image but the power of accumulated wealth.

Moses' fury upon descending the mountain and witnessing the people worshiping the calf reflects divine condemnation of idolatry. This episode is not merely a warning against polytheism but also against the obsession with material possessions, seen as a threat to genuine spiritual devotion.

"The Love of Money Is the Root of All Evil"

Paul's statement in 1 Timothy 6:10 became one of the cornerstones of biblical criticism of money. In the New Testament, Jesus also reinforces this notion by saying, *"It is easier for a camel to go through the eye of a needle than for a rich man to enter the Kingdom of Heaven"* (Matthew 19:24). These teachings shaped the worldview of many Christians, encouraging them to renounce earthly riches in favor of a simple and devout life.

Yet, while preaching humility, the Catholic Church amassed gold, land, and power. Believers were encouraged to donate their possessions in the name of salvation, while clerics enjoyed luxuries inaccessible to most. This contradiction did not go unnoticed, especially during periods like the Middle Ages.

THE MANIPULATION OF POVERTY IDEALS

The Church understood that ideological control was a powerful tool for consolidating its dominance. By preaching that money was inherently evil, it encouraged believers to relinquish their possessions, not to foster an egalitarian communal life but to enrich the institution itself.

1. **Tithes and Indulgences**
   Tithing was a moral and spiritual obligation, extracting a portion of income from peasants and nobles for the Church's coffers. Later, indulgences transformed forgiveness into a commodity, charging exorbitant sums to secure the salvation of souls.

2. **Accumulation of Land and Wealth**
   For centuries, the Church was the largest landowner in Europe, consolidating its economic and political power. This wealth was largely built through donations from believers, who thought that surrendering their assets was an act of faith.

3. **Hypocrisy in Clerical Life**
   While preaching poverty and humility, high-ranking members of the clergy lived in palaces, feasted on luxuries, and wore garments adorned with gold and precious stones. This starkly contrasted with the misery experienced by their followers.

CAPITALISM AND FAITH: A CONVENIENT ALLIANCE

With the advent of capitalism, the Church adapted its narrative to remain relevant. It began investing in businesses and markets, becoming an active participant in the system it once criticized. This reveals that the rhetoric against money was not solely spiritual but a strategy to consolidate power and influence.

CONCLUSION: MONEY AND SOCIAL CONTROL

The story of the Golden Calf and the biblical critiques of money served as a powerful tool to shape behavior, but the Church's history reveals how these teachings were subverted to enrich the institution. While condemning attachment to material goods, it established itself as one of the world's greatest economic powers.

This chapter sheds light on the inherent contradiction between preaching poverty and amassing wealth, showing how capitalism and religion often worked hand in hand to perpetuate inequality and exploit the most vulnerable.

I hope you enjoyed the book.

Thank you for your attention!